SURE Food Safety Manager Manual

For food service and retail establishments

Susan Algeo, MPH, CP-FS
George Zameska, RS, MS, CP-FS

Copyright © 2013. All rights reserved.

This manual is a guide for serving and selling safe food at food service and retail establishments. This book is not intended to be a substitute for the user's judgment and common sense. Instruis Publishing Company assumes no liability for the adherence or lack of adherence to the methods prescribed herein. Its contents have been compiled from sources believed to be reliable and represent the best information available. Any errors are unintentional.

Copyright © 2013 by Instruis Publishing Company. All rights reserved

Published by Instruis Publishing Company, Abington, Pennsylvania. Published simultaneously in Canada.

No part of this publication may be reproduced, stored in a retrieval system, or transmitted in any form or by any means, electronic, mechanical, photocopying, recording, scanning, or otherwise, except as permitted under Section 107 or 108 of the 1976 United States Copyright Act, without either the prior written permission of the Publisher. Requests to the Publisher for permission should be addressed to Instruis Publishing, Company, 1494 Old York Road, Suite 200, Abington, PA 19001, email: permissions@instruis.com.

Limit of Liability/Disclaimer of Warranty: While the publisher and authors have used their best efforts in preparing this book, they make no representations or warranties with respect to the accuracy or completeness of the contents of this book and specifically disclaim any implied warranties of merchantability of fitness for a particular purpose. No warranty may be created or extended by sales representatives or written sales materials. The advice and strategies contemplated herein may not be suitable for your situation. You should consult with a professional where appropriate. Neither the publisher nor authors shall be liable for any loss of profit or any other commercial damages, including but not limited to special, incidental, consequential, or other damages.

The Food Safety Icons are provided courtesy of the International Association for Food Protection.

Instruis Publishing Company does or may publish its books in a variety of electronic formats. Some content that appears in print may not be available in electronic books. For more information about Instruis Publishing Company products, including its SURE™ line of products, visit our web site at www.instruis.com. SURE™ is a trademark of Instruis Publishing Company.

Library of Congress Cataloging-in-Publication Data

SURE Food Safety Manager Manual/ Susan Algeo and George Zameska.

ISBN-978-0-9882914-9-2 (paper)

Instruis Publishing Company
Perfection through education.

Table of Contents

Introduction .... Page 1
Food Safety Pre-Test .... Page 3

Section 1 – Foundations of Food Safety
Chapter 1 – Regulations Overview .... Page 8
FDA Food Code .... Page 10
Foodborne Illness .... Page 10
Food Defense .... Page 11
Person-in-Charge .... Page 12
Training .... Page 13
Inspection Process .... Page 13
Crisis Management .... Page 14
Active Managerial Control .... Page 15
Flow of Food .... Page 16

Chapter 2 – Food Safety Basics .... Page 20
Hazards .... Page 22
Highly Susceptible Populations .... Page 23
FATTOM .... Page 25
Time/Temperature Control for Safety of Food – TCS Foods .... Page 27
Thermometers .... Page 28
Allergens .... Page 30

Chapter 3 – Microorganisms Challenging Food Service and Retail Establishments .... Page 36
Microorganisms .... Page 38
Naturally Occurring Chemical Hazards .... Page 42
Active Managerial Control Used to Control Microorganisms .... Page 45

Chapter 4 – Core Food Safety Features .... Page 48
Core Food Safety Features of a Food Service or Retail Establishment .... Page 50
Food Equipment and Utensils .... Page 50
Structural Components of the Establishment .... Page 52

Section 2 – Addressing the 5 CDC Risk Factors
Chapter 5 – Preventing Contamination by Proper Cleaning, Sanitizing, and Pest Control .... Page 64
Cleaning and Sanitizing Overview .... Page 66
Cleaning .... Page 66
Sanitizing .... Page 67
How to Clean and Sanitize .... Page 68
When to Clean and Sanitize .... Page 69
Cleaning Tools .... Page 69
Warewashing and Dishwashing Machines .... Page 70
Manual Warewashing and Dishwashing .... Page 70
Storage of Clean Equipment, Utensils, and Tableware .... Page 71
Pest Control .... Page 72

Storage of Chemicals .... Page 74
Chapter 6 – Applying Proper Personal Hygiene at Food Service and Retail Establishments .... Page 80
Proper Personal Hygiene Practices .... Page 82
Employee Accommodations .... Page 86
Employee Health Management and Reportable Health Illnesses .... Page 87
Procedures for Responding to Contamination Events .... Page 90
Chapter 7 - Purchasing Food from Safe Sources .... Page 96
Purchasing Food from Approved Sources .... Page 98
Food Standards .... Page 98
Foods of Special Concern .... Page 99
Receiving .... Page 100
Storing .... Page 101
Preparing .... Page 103
Chapter 8 – Proper Cooking for Food Service and Retail Establishments .... Page 112
Cooking .... Page 114
Special Cooking Considerations .... Page 116
Non-Cooking Destruction of Pathogens .... Page 118
Consumer Advisories .... Page 119
Chapter 9 – Proper Holding for Food Service and Retail Establishments .... Page 124
Hot and Cold Holding .... Page 126
Time as a Public Health Control .... Page 126
Cooling .... Page 127
Reheating .... Page 128
Serving .... Page 129
Self-Service Areas .... Page 131
Serving Food Off-Site .... Page 131

Section 3 – Proactive Food Safety System
Chapter 10 – Applying HACCP to Food Service and Retail Establishments .... Page 136
HACCP Overview .... Page 138
HACCP Principle 1: Conduct a Hazard Analysis .... Page 141
HACCP Principle 2: Determine Critical Control Points .... Page 141
HACCP Principle 3: Establish Critical Limits .... Page 142
HACCP Principle 4: Establish Monitoring Procedures .... Page 142
HACCP Principle 5: Establish Corrective Actions .... Page 143
HACCP Principle 6: Verification .... Page 143
HACCP Principle 7: Record Keeping and Documentation .... Page 144

Answer Key .... Page 149
Glossary .... Page 156
Index .... Page 156
Quick Reference Guide .... Page 163

Introduction

Our Mission

Our mission is to provide the best possible training material and support to all those who serve and sell products in the food industry. By fulfilling the mission, the food industry will minimize the risk of contamination of the food served or sold, minimize the risk of foodborne illnesses, and reduce the risk of allergic reactions to food. In studying food safety, you now are a part of the mission and have an important responsibility in continuing the mission at your food service or retail establishment.

SURE Food Safety Manual

The **SURE** *Food Safety Manager Manual* is written to provide the person-in-charge of food service and retail establishments the knowledge and skills that they will need to keep food safe. Learning and applying food safety practices in an establishment will protect customers and businesses.

The **SURE** *Food Safety Manager Manual* is designed to prepare food handlers and management for an ANSI-accredited examination. The manual was created after conducting a job-task analysis of food handlers and managers in the food service and retail industry, and surveying them about their responsibilities in serving and selling safe food.

This manual is divided into three sections:

- Section 1 – Foundations of Food Safety
- Section 2 – Addressing the Five CDC Risk Factors
- Section 3 – Proactive Food Safety System

Section 1 – Foundations of Food Safety: The person-in-charge will study an overview of the regulations, food safety basics, microorganisms that challenge food service and retail establishments, and core food safety features. This section will build the foundation that a person-in-charge will need in order to apply food safety practices.

Section 2 – Addressing the Five CDC Risk Factors: The Centers for Disease Control and Prevention (CDC) has identified the five most common causes of foodborne illness. They include purchasing food from unsafe sources, failing to cook food adequately, holding food at incorrect temperatures, using contaminated equipment, and practicing poor personal hygiene. The person-in-charge will learn how to address these issues and control these risk factors in order to be able to serve and sell safe food in their operation.

Section 3 – Proactive Food Safety System: Once a food safety foundation is built and the risk factors have been addressed, a food safety management system can be applied. Hazard Analysis and Critical Control Point (HACCP) is a proactive system that assesses the food safety hazards in an operation and identifies ways to prevent, eliminate, or reduce each hazard to a safe level. Verifying and documenting that the system is working are two essential elements to HACCP. The person-in-charge will learn to apply the seven HACCP principles in their operation.

How to Use This Book

As stated before, this manual is divided into three sections:

Section 1 – Foundations of Food Safety

Section 2 – Addressing the Five CDC Risk Factors

Section 3 – Proactive Food Safety System

Each chapter contains the following elements:

- Chapter Goals
- Myth or Fact
- Chapter Explanation
- Food for Thought
- Pop Quizzes
- Food Code Definitions
- Conclusion
- Check for Understanding
- FDA Food Code References

By reading the chapter explanations and completing the activities, the reader will be prepared to take an ANSI-accredited Food Protection Manager Examination. Being a certified food protection manager, by showing proficiency of required information through passing an accredited examination, is a requirement of the FDA Food Code and many state and local jurisdictions.

Food Safety Pre-Test

Take the Food Safety Pre-Test to measure your current food safety knowledge.
(Circle one.)

1. What is TCS?

    a. Temperature calibration sensitivity

    b. Time/temperature conduct for safety

    c. Time control sensitivity

    d. Time/temperature control for safety

2. If approved by the regulatory authority and a company, hot food can be held without temperature control for up to _____.

    a. 4 hours

    b. 5 hours

    c. 6 hours

    d. 7 hours

3. What is two-stage cooling?

    a. 135°F to 70°F (57.2°C to 21.1°C) within 4 hours and 70°F to 41°F (21.1°C to 5°C), with an additional 4 hours

    b. 135°F to 41°F (57.2°C to 5°C) in more than 4 hours

    c. 135°F to 70°F (57.2°C to 21.1°C) within 3 hours and 70°F to 41°F (21.1°C to 5°C), with an additional 2 hours

    d. 135°F to 70°F (57.2°C to 21.1°C) within 2 hours and 70°F to 41°F (21.1°C to 5°C), with an additional 4 hours

4. If approved by the regulatory authority and a company, cold food can be held without temperature control for up to _____, as long as the food does not go above 70°F (21.1°C).

    a. 4 hours

    b. 5 hours

    c. 6 hours

    d. 7 hours

5. What are the three spore-forming bacteria that cause illness?

    a. Norovirus, Salmonella, and Shigellosis

    b. Staphylococcus aureus, Clostridium bacteria, and Listeria

    c. Bacillus cereus, Clostridium botulinum, and Clostridium perfringens

    d. Cyclospora, Cryptosporidiosis, and Toxoplasmosis

6. When reheating previously cooked TCS foods for hot holding, what temperature must be reached within two hours for food that is cooked, cooled, and reheated?

    a. 135°F (57.2°C) for 15 seconds

    b. 145°F (62.7°C) for 15 seconds

    c. 155°F (68.3°C) for 15 seconds

    d. 165°F (73.9°C) for 15 seconds

Handwritten notes:
- Plant food cooled 135
- Rice, pasta, Noodle
- Seafood, steak, chops, Eggs
- Ground meat, fish, Eggs (for steam)
- Poultry, stuffed Items, turkey

7. What is the name of the written document that assesses hazards in an operation and identifies ways to prevent, eliminate, or reduce the hazards to safe levels?

    a. HACCP principle 4

    b. Standard operating procedure

    c. HACCP plan

    d. Variance

8. When reheating commercially processed foods for hot holding, what temperature must be reached?

    a. 135°F (57.2°C)

    b. 145°F (62.7°C)

    c. 155°F (68.3°C)

    d. 165°F (73.9°C)

9. What is the name of the written document that is issued by the regulatory authority that authorizes a modification or waiver of one or more requirements of the Food Code if, in the opinion of the regulatory authority, a health hazard or nuisance will not result from the modification or waiver?

    a. HACCP principle 4

    b. Standard operating procedure

    c. HACCP plan

    d. Variance

10. What is the minimum internal cooking temperature for ground meat?

    a. 135°F (57.2°C) for 15 seconds

    b. 145°F (62.7°C) for 15 seconds

    c. 155°F (68.3°C) for 15 seconds

    d. 165°F (73.9°C) for 15 seconds

11. A foodborne illness outbreak occurs when _____ or more people get sick after eating a _____ food.

    a. 20, different

    b. 2, different

    c. 20, similar

    d. 2, similar

12. A bandage found in a food is an example of which type of hazard?

    a. Biological

    b. Chemical

    c. Physical

    d. Radiological

13. Which of the following is a TCS food?

    a. Bread

    b. Mayonnaise

    c. Baked potato

    d. Chocolate

14. The most common foodborne illness is _____.
    a. E. coli
    b. Norovirus
    c. Salmonella typhi
    d. Hepatitis A

15. Handwashing stations must include which of the following?
    a. Lotion
    b. Hand antiseptics
    c. Cloth towels
    d. Handwashing sign

16. Employees are not allowed to be at work preparing food if they are _____.
    a. sneezing
    b. vomiting
    c. coughing
    d. laughing

17. Rare hamburgers cannot be served _____.
    a. on a senior menu
    b. to people with soy allergies
    c. on a children's menu
    d. to people with shellfish allergies

18. Which of the following items must be cooked to an internal temperature of 145°F (62.7°C) for 15 seconds?
    a. Steak, salmon, eggs for immediate service
    b. Hamburger, crab cakes, eggs for immediate service
    c. Stuffed poultry, salmon, eggs for hot holding
    d. Poultry, steak, eggs for hot holding

19. The temperature danger zone is _____.
    a. 42°F - 134°F (5.6°C - 56.7°C)
    b. 70°F - 125°F (21.1°C - 51.7°C)
    c. 41°F - 135°F (5 °C - 57.2°C)
    d. 41°F - 124°F (5°C - 51.1°C)

20. Verification in a HACCP plan is important because it _____.
    a. assesses the risk in the food
    b. checks the critical limit
    c. keeps documents in place
    d. confirms the plan is working as intended

How many points did you earn? _____

- **If you scored 18-20 points** – Congratulations! You are very knowledgeable already, and this should be an excellent review for you!
- **If you scored 14-17 points** – Good job! You have a basic understanding of food safety and all of its components.
- **If you scored 11-13 points** – There is no time like the present to learn about food safety! This book will give you a great opportunity to fine-tune your food safety skills.
- **If you scored 0-10 points** – Everyone needs to start somewhere! It is important to track your progress as you complete each chapter in order to earn your ANSI-accredited certification!

Chapter 1: Regulations Overview

Chapter 1: Goals

In this chapter, participants will learn to:

- Understand the role of the FDA Food Code, regulations, and the important responsibilities of the person-in-charge.
- Define food safety, foodborne illness, foodborne disease outbreak, confirmed disease outbreak, and food defense.
- Apply food safety training techniques to ensure that employees know and understand their food safety responsibilities.
- Identify an imminent health hazard as it relates to crisis management.
- Understand how active managerial control relates to the CDC risk factors.

Chapter 1: Myth or Fact

(Check one.)

1. The Food Code is the set of regulations that all food businesses must follow to operate legally.
   ✓ Myth ___ Fact

2. The Food Code represents the FDA's best advice for a uniform system of provisions that addresses the safety and protection of food offered at food service and retail operations.
   ___ Myth ✓ Fact

3. Foodborne illnesses cause very few hospitalizations and deaths in the United States per year.
   ✓ Myth ___ Fact

4. The person-in-charge (PIC) is an individual present at the food establishment who is responsible for the operation.
   ___ Myth ✓ Fact

5. Active managerial control focuses on three key operation elements: personal work practices, behavior with customers, and accurate timekeeping for employee work activities.
   ✓ Myth ___ Fact

FDA Food Code

The U.S. Food and Drug Administration (FDA) publishes the **Food Code**, a model document for safeguarding public health and ensuring that food is safe when offered to consumers. The Food Code contains practical, science-based information and provisions for mitigating risk factors known to cause foodborne illness. The FDA works with the Centers for Disease Control and Prevention (CDC), the U.S. Department of Health & Human Services (HHS), the Food Safety Inspection Service (FSIS) of the United States Department of Agriculture (USDA), and the Conference for Food Protection (CFP) to create this guidance document. Although not required, it is strongly recommended that state, county, city, and tribal agencies (local health departments) adopt the Food Code to enforce food safety regulations. By following the Food Code, food service and retail operations will decrease the risk of serving and selling contaminated food to their customers. Each establishment must follow its local regulatory agency requirements.

Foodborne Illness

A **foodborne illness** is a sickness that results from the consumption of food or beverages contaminated with disease-causing microorganisms, chemicals, or other harmful substances. A **foodborne disease outbreak** occurs when there are two or more cases of a similar illness resulting from the ingestion of a common food, also known as a foodborne illness outbreak. A **confirmed disease outbreak** is two or more cases of a similar illness in which laboratory analysis identifies a causative agent that implicates the food as the source of the illness.

The CDC estimates that there are 48 million foodborne illnesses each year in the United States, of which there are about 128,000 hospitalizations and about 3,000 deaths. Foodborne illnesses not only affect the person who is sick but also bring a great negative impact to the establishment that caused the illness. Along with the potential cost of lawsuits and insurance coverage, there could be a decrease in sales due to negative media coverage of the illness. An establishment's commitment to food safety may require extra effort, time, and cost. However, adopting a food safety culture will prevent more costly consequences.

Reportable Health Illnesses

Some foodborne illnesses are more contagious than others and can be transmitted by food handlers practicing poor personal hygiene. There are six illnesses, the "Big 6," that must be reported to the health department if an employee is diagnosed with any of them. They are:

- **H**epatitis A
- **E**. coli shiga toxin-producing
- **N**orovirus
- **S**higella
- **S**almonella typhi
- **S**almonella nontyphoidal

To reduce the risk of food handlers contaminating food, a manager must restrict or exclude employees who have symptoms such as diarrhea, vomiting, and jaundice (yellow color of the skin and whites of the eyes). Additional information and details about the Big 6 and their symptoms are explained in Chapter 6: Applying Proper Personal Hygiene at Food Service and Retail Establishments.

Food Defense

Controlling the risk factors of foodborne illness will help with **food safety**, which is the protection from unintentional contamination of food. But food service and retail establishments must also protect food from intentional contamination by applying food defense. **Food defense** is defined as the act of preventing an intentional contamination of food.

Intentional contamination could come from inside or outside the facility by:

- competitors;
- vendors;
- employees;
- customers; or
- terrorists.

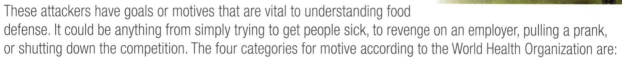

These attackers have goals or motives that are vital to understanding food defense. It could be anything from simply trying to get people sick, to revenge on an employer, pulling a prank, or shutting down the competition. The four categories for motive according to the World Health Organization are:

- disease, mass casualties, and death;
- impact on public health services;
- social and political implications; and
- economic and trade impact.

It is important that food service and retail establishments take extra precautions to defend their food and brand. The FDA recommends using the **ALERT** method for food defense.

Assure. Assure that products are purchased from safe sources.

Look. Look at areas where food is exposed and could be vulnerable.

Employees. Employees and vendors must be monitored when around food.

Reports. Reports and logs related to food defense must be maintained.

Threat. Threats must be taken seriously, and a plan must be in place if food is threatened.

By following proper food safety and food defense practices, food service and retail operations can protect their customers and their business.

Pop Quiz:
Food Defense
(Complete.)

The FDA recommends using the **ALERT** method for food defense. What action step does each letter represent?

1. A = _____

2. L = _____

3. E = _____

4. R = _____

5. T = _____

Person-in-Charge

Every food service and retail operation needs to have a designated person-in-charge. The **person-in-charge (PIC)** is an individual present at the food establishment who is responsible for the operation. A manager, supervisor, or employee with a food safety certification can be the PIC. The PIC has to be able to demonstrate knowledge of foodborne illness prevention, the application of Hazard Analysis and Critical Control Point (HACCP) principles, and the requirements of the regulatory authority. They must ensure that:

- The food establishment is approved to serve and sell food.
- Unnecessary people are not allowed in food preparation, storage, or cleaning areas.
- Employees comply with regulatory requirements.
- Employees wash their hands correctly.
- Products are inspected properly upon receiving.
- Employees cook and cool foods properly.
- Employees clean and sanitize equipment safely.
- Employees prevent bare-hand contact with ready-to-eat foods by using suitable utensils.
- Employees are trained on food safety, food allergy awareness, food defense, and HACCP.
- Food employees and conditional employees are aware of their responsibility to report health illnesses.
- Consumers are informed of the risk when ordering raw or undercooked foods.
- Consumers use clean tableware when returning to self-service areas.

  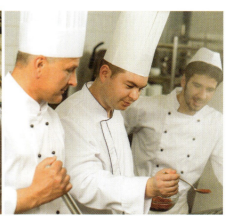

Training

A PIC must ensure that employees follow food safety practices and are properly trained on these practices. It is important that each employee be trained on food safety topics that relate to their assigned duties. Employee food safety training, specific to job duties, can be provided upon hiring, when job duties change, and continually throughout the employee's employment. Continual training is needed in order to provide employees with updates to food safety procedures and practices and to refresh their knowledge of proper food handling practices and their responsibilities.

Training can be provided by using different methods and techniques including:

- videos;
- computer-based training;
- visual aids;
- role playing;
- training manuals;
- discussions;
- demonstrations; and
- on-the-job training.

These methods can all be used to train employees on food safety. Local health departments may have specific training requirements for food employees and managers. Documentation of training is important in order to provide evidence of who was trained and when, and which topics were covered.

Inspection Process

Establishments should conduct routine self-inspections. Regulatory inspections should not be relied upon to verify the safety of the operation.

Regulatory inspections may include a review of:

- sanitation features;
- operation procedures;
- health and personal hygiene;
- CDC risk factors; and
- the flow of food.

When an inspector arrives, the PIC should confirm the inspectors identification. Then the PIC should cooperate and follow the inspector throughout the operation. It is essential to implement corrective actions while the inspector is there and immediately following the visit. The inspector will provide an inspection report to the establishment. Food service and retail establishments are required to post notification that the inspection information is available.

Crisis Management

There may be a time when a crisis does occur. A food safety crisis is an **imminent health hazard**. An imminent health hazard is a significant threat or danger to health that is considered to exist when there is evidence sufficient to show that a product, practice, circumstance, or event creates a situation that requires immediate correction or cessation of operation to prevent injury based on:

1. The number of potential injuries, and
2. The nature, severity, and duration of the anticipated injury.

An imminent health hazard may exist because of an emergency such as a fire, flood, extended interruption of electrical or water service, sewage backup, misuse of poisonous or toxic materials, onset of an apparent foodborne illness outbreak, gross insanitary occurrence or condition, or other circumstance that may endanger public health.

A PIC must be prepared to manage the crisis so the situation does not get worse. If a crisis occurs, the PIC must report the situation and the actions taken to the regulatory authority. They may need to gain permission in order to resume the operation.

When developing a crisis management plan these elements must be included: preparation, response, and recovery. Crisis management plans should include:

- Emergency contact lists;
- Power generation and lighting methods;
- Alternate water supplies (bottled water, boiled water);
- Fire suppression use and recharge;
- Food disposal or salvaging;
- Tools, equipment, cleaners, disinfectants, and methods needed for clean-up activities; and
- Alternate refrigeration (portable power generators, reefer trucks, bagged ice).

Pop Quiz:

Person-in-Charge
(Check one.)

The person-in-charge will need to:

1. Train employees concerning food safety and allergy awareness.
   ✓ Yes ___ No

2. Ensure that employees are able to touch ready-to-eat foods with bare hands.
   ___ Yes ✓ No

3. Ensure that employees know how to wash their hands.
   ✓ Yes ___ No

4. Know to have employees stop working when seriously ill.
   ✓ Yes ___ No

5. Reassure to the customers that it is safe to eat raw or undercooked foods.
   ___ Yes ✓ No

Active Managerial Control

The PIC is responsible to ensure food safety in food service and retail operations. To prevent food safety risks it is important to have procedures in place. The CDC identifies the five most significant contributing risk factors to foodborne illness as:

1. Purchasing food from unsafe sources
2. Failing to cook food adequately
3. Holding food at incorrect temperatures
4. Using contaminated equipment
5. Practicing poor personal hygiene

Active managerial control is a proactive food safety management system that creates procedures to control the CDC risk factors. The PIC must implement controls to prevent food safety violations from occurring and protect customers from the risk of foodborne illnesses. It is important that the PIC monitors what occurs in the food establishment in order to ensure that safe food handling procedures are followed. When problems or concerns arise, the PIC must effectively resolve any issues that may impact the safety of food in the food operation.

Flow of Food

The flow of food is the path that foods take from the time of purchase until the food is served or sold to the customer. Avoid time temperature abuse and cross-contamination throughout the flow of food. **Time/temperature abuse** is when food remains at an unsafe temperature for too long. **Cross-contamination** occurs when pathogens transfer from one food surface to another.

Managing temperature control of food to prevent abuse will include ensuring that:

- Food is held or stored at the correct temperature;
- Food is cooked or reheated properly;
- Food is cooled correctly;
- Thermometers are available and used to correctly and regularly check food and storage temperatures; and
- Temperatures are recorded when taken.

Managing food handling to prevent cross-contamination will require that:

- Ready-to-eat foods do not come in contact with other foods with pathogen contaminates.
    - Have raw animal foods prepared at different times.
    - Purchase prepared raw foods.
- Contaminated surfaces do not contact ready-to-eat food.
    - Use dedicated equipment for certain types of food.
    - Clean and sanitize after each task.
- Food handlers do not touch ready-to-eat food with bare hands.
- Raw animal foods of different species do not contact each other.
    - Use separate equipment.
    - Clean and sanitize equipment between uses.
    - Use proper storage practices.
    - Prepare at different times.

Flow of Food

Purchase ▼
Receive ▼
Store ▼
Prepare ▼
Cook ▼
Hold ▼
Cool ▼
Reheat ▼
Serve

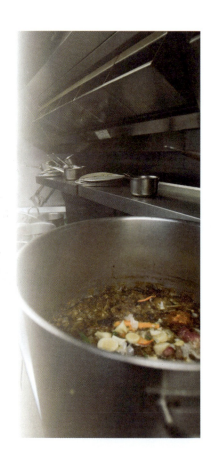

Chapter 1
Food Code Definitions

- **Confirmed disease outbreak:** a foodborne disease outbreak in which laboratory analysis of appropriate specimens identifies a causative agent, and epidemiological analysis implicates the food as the source of the illness.

- **Foodborne disease outbreak:** the occurrence of two or more cases of a similar illness resulting from the ingestion of a common food.

- **Food employee:** an individual working with unpackaged food, food equipment or utensils, or food-contact surfaces.

- **Imminent health hazard:** a significant threat or danger to health that is considered to exist when there is evidence sufficient to show that a product, practice, circumstance, or event creates a situation that requires immediate correction or cessation of operation to prevent injury based on:

    1. The number of potential injuries, and
    2. The nature, severity, and duration of the anticipated injury.

- **Person-in-charge:** the individual present at a food establishment who is responsible for the operation at the time of inspection.

Chapter 1
Conclusion

The PIC has to know their food safety responsibilities and how to ensure that employees in the food establishment follow safe food-handling practices. Employee illness poses a significant risk to the safety of food. The PIC must communicate employee responsibilities regarding reporting illness symptoms and diseases that impact food safety. The PIC needs to understand HACCP principles and how implementing active managerial control for identified food safety risks will prevent foodborne illness. The PIC must also ensure that food defense practices are used following the ALERT method.

Chapter 1

Check for Understanding
(Circle one.)

1. Active managerial control focuses on the five CDC-identified foodborne disease risk factors not including _____.
   a. purchasing food from unsafe sources
   b. failing to cook food adequately
   c. practicing poor personal hygiene
   d. failing to conduct sanitation self-inspection before operation

2. Reportable illnesses to the regulatory authority do not include which of the following _____.
   a. *Staphylococcus* skin infection
   b. *Shigella*
   c. *E. coli* O157:H7
   d. *Salmonella typhi*

3. Person-in-charge food safety responsibilities include ensuring that _____.
   a. food employee time records are accurate
   b. food employees are trained on food safety, including food allergy awareness
   c. customers always receive fresh products from the salad bar or other similar self-service area
   d. all vendor deliveries are only made by individuals who are recognized by the food operation staff members

4. Food defense is the _____.
   a. two-year supply of food for a country
   b. act of preventing the unintentional contamination of food
   c. act of preventing an intentional contamination of food
   d. none of the above

5. The U.S. Food and Drug Administration (FDA) publishes the Food Code, which is used _____.
   a. as a model document for safeguarding public health
   b. as a guidance document that establishes science-based information
   c. by state, county, city, and tribal agencies (local health departments) if adopted to enforce food safety regulations
   d. all of the above

6. Foodborne disease outbreaks are determined to occur when _____.
   a. a husband and wife share dinner, and both become ill
   b. many individuals experience the same symptoms
   c. two or more cases of a similar illness result from the ingestion of a common food
   d. two or more individuals have the same laboratory-confirmed illness

7. Which of the following can be used for food safety training?

    a. Demonstration

    b. Classroom training

    c. Discussion

    d. All of the above

8. According to the Food Code, an individual working with unpackaged food, food equipment or utensils, or food-contact surfaces is called a _____.

    a. manager

    b. team member

    c. food associate

    d. food employee

9. What is a sickness that results from the consumption of food or beverages contaminated with disease-causing microorganisms, chemicals, or other harmful substances?

    a. Foodborne outbreak

    b. Risk factor

    c. Foodborne illness

    d. Jaundice

10. Employee food safety training should be _____.

    a. provided upon hiring

    b. specific to job duties

    c. conducted continually throughout the employee's employment

    d. all of the above

FDA Food Code References

Chapter 2 – Management & Personnel
- 2-1 Supervision
    - 2-101.11 Assignment
    - 2-102.11 Demonstration
    - 2-103.11 Person-in-Charge
- 2-2 Employee Health
    - 2-201.11 Responsibility of Permit Holder, Person-in-Charge, and Conditional Employees
    - 2-201.12 Exclusions and Restrictions
    - 2-201.13 Removal, Adjustment, or Retention of Exclusions and Restrictions
- 8-4 Inspection and Correction of Violations
    - 8-404.11 Ceasing Operations and Reporting

Annex 2 – Food Defense Guidance from Farm to Table

Annex 4 – Management of Food Safety Practices – Achieving Active Managerial Control of Foodborne Illness Risk Factors

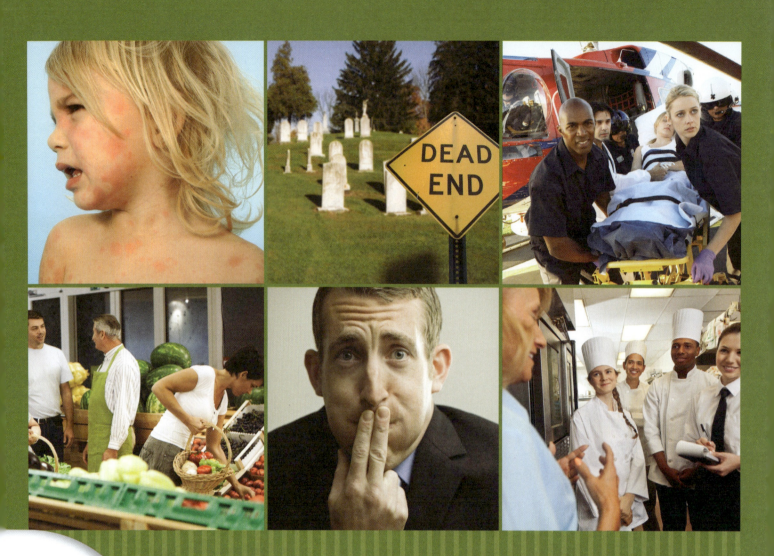

Chapter 2:
Food Safety Basics

Chapter 2: Goals

In this chapter, participants will learn to:

- Define the three types of hazards that can impact food safety.
- Understand people in the highly susceptible population.
- Identify the conditions that support pathogen growth and survival.
- Apply calibration techniques to ensure accuracy of thermometers used for checking food and equipment operating temperatures.
- Recognize the major food allergens.
- Identify the foods that require time/temperature control for safety and the flow of food.

Chapter 2: Myth or Fact

(Check one.)

1. Biological hazards are only of concern when foods are not being cooked to kill pathogens.
   ✓ Myth ___ Fact

2. Metal shavings from opening a can are not a physical hazard because the shavings can be seen and removed to maintain the safety of the opened food.
   ✓ Myth ___ Fact

3. A food operation cannot do anything that will change the FATTOM condition or characteristic of a particular food.
   ✓ Myth ___ Fact

4. People with food allergies will be kept safe as long as they do not come in contact with the allergen.
   ___ Myth ✓ Fact

5. People with weakened immune systems can eat the same food as everyone else without risk of getting ill.
   ✓ Myth ___ Fact

Hazards

A **hazard** is a biological, chemical, or physical property that may cause an unacceptable consumer health risk, such as illness or injury.

Biological Hazards

Biological hazards are harmful microorganisms that include viruses, bacteria, fungi, and parasites. These are also known as pathogens. Pathogens can be transferred from person to person, person to food, person to food contact surface, or food to food. Once consumed, these pathogens can cause illness.

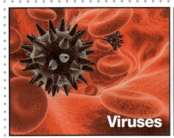
Viruses

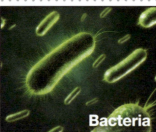
Bacteria

Fungi

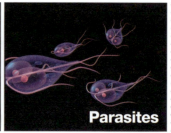
Parasites

Chemical Hazards

Chemical hazards can come from a variety of different sources [pewter (Lead)] and can be naturally occurring or added to foods. Chemical hazards can cause illness or injury within minutes when consumed and include the following examples:

Chemical Hazards Added to Foods	Naturally Occurring Chemical Hazards
• Toxic metals (lead, copper, and zinc/galvanized)	• Food allergens
• Unsafe plastics or other materials	• Plant toxins
• Sanitation chemicals (cleaners and sanitizers)	• Mushroom toxins
• Maintenance chemicals (polishes and lubricants)	• Shellfish toxins
• Pesticides	• Fish and other seafood toxins

It is important to prevent chemical hazards that cause illness or injury due to improper use or contamination. To decrease the likelihood of a chemical hazard occurring, the following practices are required:

- Purchase foods from approved sources;
- Use approved equipment and utensils;
- Know ingredients used in foods;
- Follow manufacturer instructions on proper chemical use and disposal;
- Label all containers used to store or hold chemicals removed from original containers; and
- Store chemicals away from or below food to prevent accidental use, spillage or leakage into foods.

Physical Hazards

Physical hazards are foreign objects not expected to be in food that can cause harm to the consumer.

Common Physical Hazards				
Glass	Bandages	Bolts	Bugs	Fruit pits
Metal shavings	Hair	Nuts	Packaging	Dirt
Staples	Jewelry	Screws	Plastic wrap	Bones

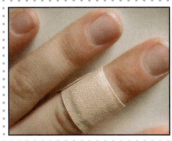

To decrease the likelihood of a physical hazard occurring:

- Practice good personal hygiene;
- Protect or cover foods during handling;
- Maintain the physical environment and equipment;
- Purchase food from safe sources; and
- Inspect food that is being received and served.

Highly Susceptible Populations

People in **highly susceptible populations** have weaker immune systems than people in the general population. People with weaker immune systems can get sick from a smaller number of pathogens. People with compromised immune systems can also have more serious medical consequences than people who are not immunocompromised.

Highly susceptible populations include:

- **Older adults**
  - Immune systems are weakening due to age and are not as capable of providing protection against disease
- **Preschool-aged children**
  - Immune systems are still developing
- **Immunocompromised people**
  - Immune systems are dysfunctional or weakened due to medication use or a medical condition (organ transplant, diabetes, cancer, HIV, Crohn's disease, and/or others)

Pregnant women are at high risk for acquiring listeriosis, an infection caused by *Listeria monocytogenes* bacteria. This infection can transfer to an unborn baby and cause its death.

Pop Quiz:

Highly Susceptible Populations
(Check one.)

Highly susceptible populations refer to people who have a weakened immune system and includes which of the following:

1. 85-year-old male living in a nursing home
   ✓ Yes ___ No

2. 4-year-old preschool child
   ✓ Yes ___ No

3. 29-year-old person using chemotherapy drugs
   ✓ Yes ___ No

4. 74-year-old healthy woman living in her own home
   ✓ Yes ___ No

5. 11-year-old sixth grade student
   ___ Yes ✓ No

FATTOM

FATTOM represents the six environmental conditions that are needed for microorganisms to grow and survive: Food, Acidity, Time, Temperature, Oxygen, and Moisture. Biological hazards, particularly bacteria, need the right FATTOM conditions in order to grow and survive. Each pathogen requires specific FATTOM conditions to grow. When these conditions are altered, unwanted pathogen growth can be prevented.

Specifics about these conditions include:

- **Food**
  - Protein and carbohydrates in foods provide pathogens with nutrients needed to grow. Many foods have these nutrients.

- **Acidity**
  - Acidity is measured on a pH scale from 0-14. Many pathogens grow in foods with a pH between 4.6 and 7.5. Most foods are found in this pH range.

- **Time**
  - The longer the food is in the Temperature Danger Zone (TDZ), the greater the opportunity for pathogens to grow. Food in the TDZ for more than 4 hours risks having pathogens reach unsafe levels or produce harmful toxins.

- **Temperature**
  - Pathogens grow in the TDZ of 41°F-135°F (5°C-57.2°C). They grow best at temperatures between 70°F-125°F (21.1°C-51.7°C).

- **Oxygen**
  - The oxygen levels available will impact which pathogens can grow. Some require oxygen to grow. Some cannot have oxygen to grow. Other pathogens can survive either with or without oxygen.

- **Moisture**
  - Water is needed for pathogens to grow and survive. Water in foods is measured as water activity (a_w) on a scale of 0-1. Pathogens will grow in foods with water activity levels above 0.85.

FOOD FOR THOUGHT

FATTOM

When FATTOM conditions support growth, pathogens can reach unsafe levels, resulting in foodborne illness when food is consumed.

- **Food** – The concept and food choices will determine whether food will support microorganism growth.

- **Acidity** – Adding acid, such as vinegar, to food can lower the pH to prevent pathogen growth.

- **Time** – Monitoring food temperature and limiting the amount of time foods are in the TDZ will prevent pathogen growth.

- **Temperature** – Keeping foods hot or cold, out of the TDZ, will prevent growth.

- **Oxygen** – Opening a package can expose food to oxygen. Sealing packages using special processes can exclude oxygen. Certain cooking processes can change a food's oxygen environment. Oxygen environment changes can affect the growth of pathogens and the types of pathogens that will be able to grow.

- **Moisture** – Removing moisture from foods by drying and baking, or adding salt or sugar can limit or stop the growth of pathogens. Adding water to dry foods provides moisture for pathogen growth. Pathogen growth can be controlled by not adding water to a dry food until needed for use.

The PIC of the food operation has the responsibility of ensuring that proper food handling practices are followed in order to limit the FATTOM conditions for pathogen growth. This is especially important for foods that require time/temperature control for safety of food (TCS).

Pop Quiz:

FATTOM
(Check all that apply.)

FATTOM represents the six environmental conditions that are needed in order for microorganisms to grow and survive and includes the following:

1. ✓ Acidity
2. ✓ Temperature
3. ___ Toxin
4. ___ Movement
5. ✓ Food
6. ___ Foreign object
7. ✓ Time
8. ___ Activity
9. ✓ Moisture
10. ✓ Oxygen

Time/Temperature Control for Safety of Food – TCS Foods

TCS foods have FATTOM conditions that support pathogen growth and toxin formation unless they are kept out of temperature danger zone. Therefore, these foods need **time/temperature control for safety (TCS)** to prevent pathogenic microorganism growth or toxin formation.

TCS foods include:

- Meat (beef, pork, veal, and lamb);
- Poultry (chicken, turkey, and duck);
- Eggs*;
- Fish;
- Shellfish;
- Dairy;
- Baked potatoes;
- Heat-treated plant food;
- Raw sprout and sprout seeds;
- Tofu (soy products);
- Untreated garlic and oil mixtures; and
- Cut leafy greens, cut melons, cut tomatoes, or mixtures of cut tomatoes.

Ready-to-eat (RTE) food is food that is edible without additional preparation. RTE food will not receive any treatment to make the food safe. This includes cooked foods, salads, condiments, and baked goods. RTE foods need to be protected from contamination. An important contamination control measure for RTE foods is to not have bare-hand contact.

* Pasteurized shell eggs are heat treated to eliminate *Salmonella*. Pasteurized shell eggs are not a TCS food. These eggs would be designated with an icon as pictured.

Thermometers

Maintaining food at safe temperatures out of the TDZ requires monitoring. Thermometer requirements may differ for food and equipment. The PIC must follow manufacturer's directions when using thermometers. The directions vary for use, storage, and on how to properly handle each thermometer. A thermometer is a utensil and must be properly cleaned and sanitized. Thermometers and other temperature recording devices used to monitor food and equipment temperature include:

Thermometer Type	Use	Special Features	Limiting Factors	Advantage
Bi-metallic stemmed thermometer	Internal food and environment (air and water)	Simple manual non-electronic device Pocket size and larger Probe and immersion-style probes	Slow response With or without calibration ability Probe tip or stem immersion reading types Thin foods difficult to test	Low cost
Thermocouple and thermistor thermometers	Internal food and environment (air and water)	Digital readings Multiple interchangeable probes • Penetration • Immersion • Surface • Air Electronic data capture and transmission capability	Higher cost Special calibration requirements	High accuracy Fast response time
Infrared (IR) non-contact thermometer	Surface temperatures	Laser indicator option for surface area location being monitored	Spot to distance ratio is an important parameter for IR thermometer selection and use Additional thermometers required for product or environment monitoring	Very fast temperature survey tool
Time-temperature indicator	Ambient environment	Physical visible color change indicates specific target temperature exceeded or met	Single use, disposable	Low cost (Transportation monitoring tool, dish machine water temperature monitoring)
Data logger	Food or ambient environment	Electronic data capture for transmission or download to computer or other reporting system	Requires computer or other electronic data capture and report generation device	Provides historical time-based data for use and assessment (Transportation monitoring tool)
Minimum/maximum registering thermometer	Internal food and environment (air and water)	Indicates lowest or highest temperature achieved	Waterproof seal maintenance required	Measure temperature in environments that can have rapid changes (Water temperature measurement in dish machine)
Continuous recorder	Internal food and environment (air and water)	Non-electronic or electronic data capture to create physical and electronic records	Non-portable units installed for specific equipment or location	Alarm and electronic notice or communication capable portable sensors

Accuracy and Calibration

Food thermometers need to be accurate to within ±2°F (±1°C). Equipment air and water temperature measuring devices need to be accurate to within ±3°F (±1.5°C).

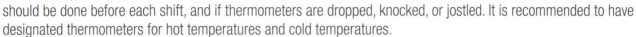

Calibrating temperature measuring devices is done to ensure constant accuracy and reliability. Thermometer calibration needs to be done in accordance with manufacturer's specifications. This may require calibration by the manufacturer. To ensure accuracy, manual calibration should be done before each shift, and if thermometers are dropped, knocked, or jostled. It is recommended to have designated thermometers for hot temperatures and cold temperatures.

Accurate calibration for a bi-metallic stemmed thermometer can be done by one of two ways: ice-point method or boiling-point method.

Ice-Point Method

Step 1: Fill a container with crushed ice and water.

Step 2: Submerge sensing area of stem or probe for 30 seconds or until indicator needle stops moving.

Step 3: Hold calibration nut and rotate thermometer head until it reads 32°F (0°C).

Boiling-Point Method

Step 1: Bring a deep pan of water to a boil.

Step 2: Submerge sensing area of stem or probe for 30 seconds or until indicator needle stops moving.

Step 3: Hold calibration nut and rotate thermometer head until it reads 212°F (100°C) at sea level.

Allergens

Food allergens are a chemical hazard and an important part of food safety. Allergy symptoms occur when a person's immune system has a negative reaction to a food or food ingredient. The effects can be minor or severe. Severe allergic reactions can quickly escalate to serious physical reactions that can lead to death. Although a person can be allergic to almost any food, these eight foods, called the "Big 8" allergens, account for 90% or more of all food allergies in the United States. These allergens are:

- Milk;
- Eggs;
- Fish (such as bass, flounder, or cod);
- Crustacean shellfish (such as crab, lobster, or shrimp);
- Soybeans;
- Wheat;
- Peanuts; and
- Tree nuts (such as almonds, pecans, or walnuts).

Packaged food must declare in the ingredient section of the product label what allergens are present.

Allergic reactions can affect different systems in a person's body and cause different symptoms:

Allergy Symptoms

Body system	Skin	Gastrointestinal	Respiratory	Cardiovascular	Anaphylaxis (a severe reaction to food that affects two or more systems)
Symptoms	• Hives • Eczema • Rash • Swelling of lips, face, or tongue	• Stomach cramps • Nausea • Vomiting • Diarrhea	• Wheezing • Nasal congestion • Trouble breathing	• Dizziness • Lightheaded • Fainting	• Swelling that causes air passages to be blocked • Shock • Loss of consciousness • Death

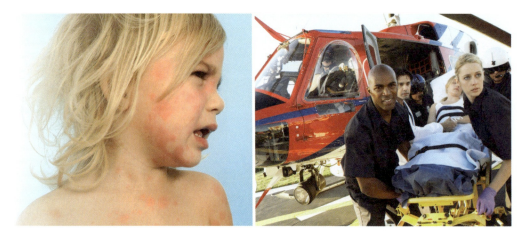

To avoid these reactions, a food service or retail establishment must be aware of ingredients and prevent cross-contact. Cross-contact is when an allergen transfers from one food or surface to another. The PIC must inform both front-of-house and back-of-house personnel of their responsibilities as they relate to allergens.

Front-of-House

- Ask customers about any allergies.
- Be able to describe dishes and tell customers all ingredients used.
- Do not serve or sell food to a customer if the allergen is in, on, or comes in contact with the item.

Back-of-House

- Wash hands and change gloves before preparing food for customers with an allergy.
- Use clean and sanitized equipment and serving utensils.
- Cook allergen food in separate fryer(s).

Front-of-House   Back-of-House

Assisting Customers with Allergens

- Notify the PIC.
- Serve customers with allergens using different color plates.
- Use separate slips for orders.
- Color code food preparation equipment.
- Ensure that all foods are appropriately identified with labels, posters, or signs.

Never guess or assume when there is a question about food allergies. If unsure of ingredients or preparation procedures for particular items, offer the customer something else that is safe. If the operation cannot assure that foods are safe from a particular allergen, the customer must be informed.

Chapter 2
Food Code Definitions

- **a_w:** water activity is a measure of the free moisture in a food, is the quotient of the water vapor pressure of the substance divided by the vapor pressure of pure water at the same temperature, and is indicated by the symbol a_w.

- **Hazard:** a biological, chemical, or physical property that may cause an unacceptable consumer health risk.

- **Highly susceptible population:** persons who are more likely than other people in the general population to experience foodborne disease because they are:
(1) Immunocompromised; preschool-aged children, or older adults; and
(2) Obtaining food at a facility that provides services such as custodial care, health care, or assisted living, such as a child or adult day care center, kidney dialysis center, hospital or nursing home, or nutritional or socialization services such as a senior center.

- **Major food allergen:**
(a) Milk, eggs, fish (such as bass, flounder, and cod, and including crustacean shellfish such as crab, lobster, or shrimp), tree nuts (such as almonds, pecans, or walnuts), wheat, peanuts, and soybeans; or
(b) A food ingredient that contains protein derived from a food, as specified in subparagraph (a) of this definition.

- **pH:** the symbol for the negative logarithm of the hydrogen ion concentration, which is a measure of the degree of acidity or alkalinity of a solution. Values between 0 and 7 indicate acidity, and values between 7 and 14 indicate alkalinity. The value for pure distilled water is 7, which is considered neutral.

- **Risk:** the likelihood that an adverse health effect will occur within a population as a result of a hazard in a food.

Chapter 2
Conclusion

The PIC will need to apply knowledge of biological, chemical, or physical food safety hazards to prevent harm or illness that can result from these hazards. Effective monitoring of food conditions to control growth or survival of biological hazards will require use of accurately calibrated equipment. Exercising these control measures can be even more important when individuals who are in a highly susceptible population group are being served. Food safety risks due to food allergens will require the PIC to implement careful review of all food ingredients, employee food preparation, and handling procedures to minimize food allergen risks to customers.

Chapter 2

Check for Understanding

(Circle one.)

1. _____ hazards are harmful microorganisms.

    a. Biological

    b. Chemical

    c. Physical

    d. Electrical

2. Foods that contain "Big 8" allergens include all but _____.

    a. chocolate chip cookies

    b. cheese and crackers

    c. green salad with oil and vinegar

    d. fish and chips

3. FATTOM conditions that are easiest to exercise control over in the food operation are _____.

    a. temperature and moisture

    b. temperature and acidity

    c. temperature and time

    d. temperature and oxygen

4. Food monitoring thermometers can be checked for accuracy using the _____ method.

    a. ice-check

    b. hot-water

    c. ice-point

    d. hot-point

5. Allergic reactions can be prevented by _____.

    a. controlling time

    b. avoiding cross-contact

    c. controlling temperature

    d. avoiding physical hazards

6. Physical hazards do not include _____.

    a. hair and bandages

    b. bleeding cuts on the hands

    c. accumulated dust on wires and piping over food preparation areas

    d. unprotected intact lights over food areas

7. TCS foods require _____.

    a. time control for safety

    b. temperature control for safety

    c. time and temperature control for safety

    d. time control for storage

8. To prevent chemical hazards, always _____.

    a. follow label instructions for use

    b. store chemicals away from foods

    c. test sanitizer solution concentration strength using a test kit

    d. all of the above

9. Thermometers used for checking food temperature must be accurate to _____.

    a. ±1°F (±2°C)

    b. ±2°F (±1°C)

    c. ±3°F (±1.5°C)

    d. ±1.5°F (±3°C)

10. Who would be most susceptible to a foodborne illness?

    a. A 45 year old woman

    b. A 25 year old man

    c. A person with cancer

    d. A person with young children

FDA Food Code References

Chapter 4 – Equipment, Utensils & Linens

    • 4-2 Design and Construction

        ○ 4-203.11 Temperature Measuring Devices, Food

        ○ 4-203.12 Temperature Measuring Devices, Ambient Air and Water

Chapter 3:
Microorganisms Challenging Food Service and Retail Establishments

Chapter 3: Goals

In this chapter, participants will learn to:

- Define the different types of microorganisms associated with food safety and biological hazards.
- Identify viruses, bacteria, parasites, fungi, and toxins.
- Identify likely food sources for different food pathogens.
- Apply specific food safety practices to limit risk of foodborne disease from specific microorganisms.
- Understand how the PIC manages microorganisms in a food service or retail establishment through employee health policies and standard operating procedures.
- Recognize the importance of establishing active managerial control for preventing risk factors.

Chapter 3: Myth or Fact

(Check one.)

1. Microorganisms, "small living things," can get people sick when eaten or ingested.
   ___Myth ✓Fact

2. Pathogens are not found in produce from local farmers.
   ✓Myth ___Fact

3. Pathogens include bacteria, viruses, fungi, and parasites, which can be naturally found in food.
   ___Myth ✓Fact

4. The person-in-charge (PIC) is an individual present at the food service or retail establishment who is responsible for controlling patron exposure to food pathogens.
   ___Myth ✓Fact

5. Pathogens can be transferred from person to person, person to food, or food to food.
   ___Myth ✓Fact

Microorganisms

Biological hazards are harmful microorganisms known as pathogens. Foods can be contaminated by pathogens from animals, humans, soil, and water. In food service and retail operations, the types of microorganisms that cause biological hazards and affect food safety include:

- Viruses;
- Bacteria;
- Parasites; and
- Fungi (molds, yeasts, mushrooms).

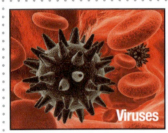
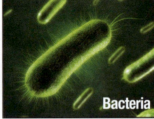
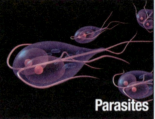

Microorganisms typically cannot be seen, smelled, or tasted. Microorganisms are potentially present throughout the flow of food and in all areas of the food service and retail establishment. This is why the PIC must have employee health policies and standard operating procedures that are:

- established;
- implemented;
- followed;
- monitored; and
- verified

in order to prevent, eliminate, or reduce microorganisms to a safe level.

Biological hazards are often the greatest concern due to their potential to create illness. The PIC must ensure that controls are in place to prevent the spread of illness and to protect employees, vendors, customers, and the public. If policies and procedures are not followed, then the likelihood of the spread of illness increases significantly.

Pathogens can be transferred from person to person, person to food, person to food contact surface, or food to food. Once consumed, these pathogens, or toxic substances they produced, can cause a foodborne illness. Microorganisms can cause illness in three basic ways.

1. **Infection** – microorganism enters the body and grows, causing illness. — *Salemon*

2. **Intoxication or poisoning** – microorganism-created toxin, a toxic or poisonous substance, that when ingested causes illness.

3. **Toxin-mediated infection** – microorganism in the body produces a toxin that causes illness.

E-coli

Viruses

Viruses are the smallest of the pathogens and can only replicate inside living cells of an organism. They can be found on a food, but will not grow in the food. Viruses that cause many of the foodborne illnesses are found in the intestines and as a result are most often spread through a fecal-hand-oral route. Practicing good personal hygiene will be the most important preventative measure for not causing foodborne illness from viruses. The two viruses that are the most significant are Hepatitis A and Norovirus. These viruses are shown in the following chart.

Virus	Food Source	Symptoms	Onset Time	Prevention
Hepatitis A (THE BIG 6)	• Ready-to-eat foods • Shellfish from contaminated water • Contaminated drinking water	• Fever • Headache • Nausea • Abdominal pain • Jaundice	15-50 days	• Practice good personal hygiene • Exclude employees with Hepatitis A or jaundice • Purchase shellfish from approved suppliers
Norovirus (THE BIG 6)	• Ready-to-eat foods • Shellfish from contaminated water • Contaminated drinking water	• Diarrhea • Fever • Headache • Nausea • Abdominal pain • Vomiting	12-48 hours	• Practice good personal hygiene • Exclude employees with Norovirus, vomiting, and diarrhea • Purchase shellfish from approved suppliers

Viruses

Norovirus has been identified as the leading cause of foodborne illness in the United States. Both Hepatitis A and Norovirus are considered to be very contagious. If an employee is diagnosed with either of these viruses, it must be reported to the health department.

Bacteria

Bacteria are unicellular microorganisms that can grow in people and in food. If not controlled, they can grow to an unsafe level or produce toxins and cause a foodborne illness. Controlling for time and temperature is the most important preventative measure. Bacteria can be found as part of the food itself, or it can spread through contaminated water, or by people through the fecal-hand-oral route. The following chart lists many common bacteria responsible for causing foodborne illness.

Bacteria	Food Source	Symptoms	Onset Time	Prevention
Bacillus cereus	• Cooked rice dishes • Meats • Stews • Gravies	• Abdominal cramps • Watery diarrhea • Nausea	10-16 hours	• Control time and/or temperature
Campylobacter jejuni	• Poultry	• Abdominal pain • Diarrhea • Fever • Cramping	2-5 days	• Control time and/or temperature
Clostridium botulinum (botulism)	• Improperly canned foods • Baked potatoes in foil • ROP foods	• Diarrhea • Blurred vision • Difficulty swallowing • Respiratory failure • Vomiting	12-72 hours	• Control time and/or temperature • Inspect packaging
Clostridium perfringens	• Meats • Stews • Gravies • Pre-cooked foods	• Watery diarrhea • Intense abdominal cramps	8-16 hours	• Control time and/or temperature
Escherichia coli (E. coli) - Shiga toxin-producing (THE BIG 6)	• Ground beef • Unpasteurized milk and juice • Raw fruits and vegetables (sprouts) • Contaminated water	• Severe diarrhea (often bloody) • Abdominal pain • Vomiting • Kidney failure	1-8 days	• Control time and/or temperature • Practice good personal hygiene • Exclude employees with E. coli or diarrhea
Listeria monocytogenes (listeriosis)	• Ready-to-eat deli meats • Unpasteurized milk • ROP foods	• Diarrhea • Fever • Nausea • Muscle aches • Stillbirth in pregnant women	9-48 hours for gastro-intestinal symptoms; 2-6 weeks for invasive disease	• Control time and/or temperature • Avoid unpasteurized milk • Throw out product past expiration date
Salmonella species (nontyphoidal salmonellosis) (THE BIG 6)	• Poultry • Eggs • Unpasteurized milk or juice • Contaminated raw fruits and vegetables	• Diarrhea • Fever • Abdominal cramps • Vomiting	6-48 hours	• Control time and/or temperature
Salmonella typhi (typhoid fever – salmonellosis) (THE BIG 6)	• Ready-to-eat foods • Beverages	• Fever • Headache • Abdominal cramps • Weakness	24-72 hours	• Control time and/or temperature • Practice good personal hygiene • Exclude employees with Salmonella typhi
Shigella species (shigellosis – bacterial dysentery) (THE BIG 6)	• Salads with TCS foods (chicken, tuna, potato, pasta salads) • Raw produce	• Diarrhea • Abdominal cramps • Fever	4-7 days	• Control time and/or temperature • Practice good personal hygiene • Control flies in operation • Exclude employees with Shigellosis
Staphylococcus aureus (staph food poisoning)	• Salads with TCS foods (chicken, tuna, potato, pasta salads) • Raw produce	• Severe nausea • Abdominal cramps • Vomiting	1-6 hours	• Control time and/or temperature • Practice good personal hygiene • Cover wounds

FOOD FOR THOUGHT

Bacteria

E. coli, Salmonella typhi, and *shigella* infections are all considered to be highly contagious. If an employee is diagnosed with any of these bacteria-caused illnesses, it must be reported to the health department.

Some bacteria are "spore formers," which create a protective shield around themselves to withstand harsh environmental conditions such as lack of water or low and high temperatures. Bacteria spores can be in the soil and can naturally contaminate produce and animals that are exposed to the soil or dust. The spore-forming bacteria are *Bacillus cereus, Clostridium botulinum,* and *Clostridium perfringens*. Normal cooking or freezing does not kill the spore form of bacteria. Once food is cooled to a dangerous temperature, the spore-forming bacteria can begin to grow and multiply, so it is important to control time and temperature during the preparing, cooling, reheating, and holding of food.

Some customers may choose to consume animal foods raw, undercooked, or without eliminating pathogens. This is why a written statement concerning a health risk is needed.

Methicillin-resistant *Staphylococcus aureus* (MRSA) is a strain of the staph bacteria that is resistant to most medications. It can cause skin infections in the general population. In health care settings, MRSA can be much more severe and life threatening, causing bloodstream infections and pneumonia.

Pop Quiz:

Bacteria
(Complete.)

Match the bacteria with its common food source by placing the correct letter in the blank provided.

Bacteria

1. __d__ Shigella   *salad, flies*
2. __e__ Salmonella nontyphoidal   *(poultry eggs)*
3. __c__ E. coli
4. __b__ Botulism
5. __a__ Listeria

Food Source

a. Deli meats
b. Improperly canned foods
c. Undercooked beef
d. Tuna salad
e. Poultry

uncooked fish / Game animal

Parasites

A **parasite** is an organism that lives on or in a host organism and gets its food from, or at the expense of, its host. Parasites are found most often in seafood and contaminated water. They can also be found in wild game and livestock animals. Food safety parasites can be larger organisms, such as worms, that can be easily seen, or can be small, requiring a microscope to see them clearly. Contaminated water can be a source of parasites and can spread through agricultural crop production. Cooking or freezing foods can kill parasites. The following chart highlights a few of the most significant parasites associated with illness from foods.

Parasite	Food Source	Symptoms	Onset Time	Prevention
Anisakis simplex (anisakiasis)	• Raw or undercooked fish	• Tingling in mouth and throat • Coughing up worms	1-14 days	• Purchase fish from approved suppliers • Cook fish to minimum internal cooking temperature • Freeze fish for proper time and temperature
Cryptosporidium parvum (cryptosporidiosis)	• Contaminated water • Produce	• Fever • Nausea • Abdominal cramps • Vomiting • Dehydration • Weight loss	2-10 days	• Purchase from approved suppliers • Practice good personal hygiene
Giardia lamblia (giardiasis)	• Contaminated water • Produce	• Diarrhea • Intestinal Gas • Nausea • Abdominal cramps • Vomiting • Dehydration	7-15 days	• Purchase from approved suppliers • Practice good personal hygiene

Fungi: Molds, Yeasts, and Mushrooms

Another group of pathogens is fungi, including molds, yeasts, and mushrooms. **Fungi** are often spoilage microorganisms that may not always cause illnesses, but can cause a food to spoil. Many fungi produce toxins that can be carcinogenic, cause acute illness, and even death. This is particularly true when it comes to wild poisonous mushrooms that can be mistaken for edible safe varieties. Molds that commonly spoil foods can also produce harmful toxins.

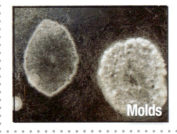

Naturally Occurring Chemical Hazards

Toxins: Mushroom Toxins, Fish Toxins, Shellfish Toxins, and Plant Toxins

Naturally occurring toxins in certain types of mushrooms, fish, shellfish, and plants can cause serious illnesses and are potentially deadly when consumed. Most toxins are not destroyed by cooking or freezing. Purchasing food from approved sources is the responsibility of the PIC in order to limit risks from these toxins. These items must also be inspected upon delivery, and received with the proper documentation from the supplier. The following chart highlights fish and shellfish toxins.

Toxin Illness	Food Source	Symptoms	Onset Time	Prevention
Scombroid or histamine fish poisoning (scombrotoxin)	• Tuna, mackerel, bonito, mahi mahi, bluefish, jack fish, amberjack, herring, sardine and other species	• Rash, diarrhea, flushing, sweating, headache, and vomiting • Burning or swelling of the mouth, abdominal pain, or a metallic taste may also occur	2 minutes - 2 hours	• Purchase from approved suppliers
Ciguatera poisoning (ciguatoxin)	• Tropical reef fish – grouper, sea bass, snapper, mullet, barracuda *Amber Jack*	• Nausea, vomiting, diarrhea, cramps, excessive sweating, headache, and muscle aches • The sensation of burning or pins and needles, weakness, itching, and dizziness can occur • Reversal of temperature sensation in the mouth (hot surfaces feeling cold and cold, hot), unusual taste sensations, nightmares, or hallucinations	A few minutes - 6 hours Up to 30 hours	• Purchase from approved suppliers
Paralytic shellfish poisoning (saxitoxin)	• Mussels, cockles, clams, scallops, oysters, crabs, and lobsters	• Numbness or tingling of the face, arms, and legs • Headache, dizziness, nausea, and muscular incoordination • Muscle paralysis and respiratory failure, death in 2 to 25 hours	15 minutes - 10 hours Normally within 2 hours	• Purchase from approved suppliers
Diarrhetic shellfish poisoning (okadaic acid toxin)	• Mussels, oysters, clams, scallops, and cockles	• Vomiting, diarrhea, body aches, fever, and chills	2-15 hours	• Purchase from approved suppliers
Neurotoxic shellfish poisoning (brevetoxin)	• Oysters, clams, and mussels	• Numbness, tingling in the mouth, arms and legs, incoordination, and gastrointestinal upset • Reversal of temperature sensation in the mouth	1-3 hour(s)	• Purchase from approved suppliers
Amnesic shellfish poisoning (domoic acid)	• Crabs, oysters, clams, and mussels	• Gastrointestinal distress • Dizziness, headache, disorientation, and permanent short-term memory loss • In severe poisoning, seizures, paralysis, and death	24 hours-days	• Purchase from approved suppliers

As seen in the charts, microorganisms can cause many different symptoms, and the highly susceptible population will be at a higher risk for these symptoms. A **risk** is the likelihood that an adverse health effect will occur within a population as a result of a hazard in a food. Sometimes people may be asymptomatic. **Asymptomatic** is defined as without obvious symptoms; not showing or producing indications of a disease or other medical condition, such as an individual infected with a pathogen but not exhibiting or producing any signs or symptoms of vomiting, diarrhea, or jaundice. Asymptomatic people can be carriers and spread pathogens unknowingly.

Pop Quiz:

PIC Managing Microorganisms
(Check one.)

The person-in-charge of a food service or retail establishment will need to do which of the following in order to manage microorganisms.

1. Ensure that employees know how to wash their hands in order to stop the spread of microorganisms.
   ✓ Yes ___ No

2. Train employees to identify likely sources of viruses and bacteria.
   ✓ Yes ___ No

3. Ensure that employees only serve ready-to-eat foods with less than an inch of mold on them.
   ___ Yes ✓ No

4. Ensure that customers know it is safe to eat foods that contain parasites.
   ___ Yes ✓ No

5. Have employees stop working when seriously ill with a virus.
   ✓ Yes ___ No

Active Managerial Control Used to Control Microorganisms

Microorganisms can be controlled by applying **active managerial control** – a proactive food safety management system that creates procedures to control the five CDC risk factors.

For example, active managerial control can be achieved by:

CDC Risk Factor		Example Control
	Purchasing food from unsafe sources	Purchase shellfish from approved suppliers with proper identification to reduce the risk of Amnesic shellfish poisoning.
	Failing to cook foods adequately	Cook ground beef to the proper internal cooking temperature to reduce the risk of E. coli.
	Holding foods at incorrect temperatures 41↓ 135↑	Hold salads with TCS foods below cold holding temperature requirements to reduce the risk of Shigella.
	Using contaminated equipment	Clean and sanitize cutting boards after preparing raw chicken to reduce the risk of Salmonellosis.
	Practicing poor personal hygiene	Employees must be excluded from work if they are vomiting or have diarrhea in order to reduce the risk of Hepatitis A.

Chapter 3
Food Code Definitions

- **Asymptomatic:** without obvious symptoms; not showing or producing indications of a disease or other medical condition, such as an individual infected with a pathogen but not exhibiting or producing any signs or symptoms of vomiting, diarrhea, or jaundice. Asymptomatic includes not showing symptoms because symptoms have resolved or subsided, or because symptoms never manifested.
- **Hazard:** a biological, chemical, or physical property that may cause an unacceptable consumer health risk.
- **Risk:** the likelihood that an adverse health effect will occur within a population as a result of a hazard in a food.

Chapter 3
Conclusion

The PIC of a food service or retail establishment has to ensure that customers and food employees are not at risk from illnesses that can easily be spread through food or people. The PIC recognizes that certain foods can create specific concerns regarding safety and that ill food employees also can be of concern for food contamination from specific pathogens. By being knowledgeable about the sources of pathogens and associated control measures to prevent illness, the PIC can ensure that necessary actions are taken to reduce the risk of foodborne disease transmission.

Chapter 3
Check for Understanding
(Circle one.)

1. Foodborne disease pathogens will cause all of the following except _____.
    a. intoxication or poisoning
    b. toxin-mediated infection
    c. organic infection
    d. infection

2. Which control is used to reduce the risk of Norovirus?
    a. Washing hands after preparing food
    b. Cooking shellfish to minimum cooking temperatures
    c. Washing hands before preparing food
    d. Holding lunch meats below required holding temperatures

3. E. coli is most often found in _____.
    a. raw ground beef
    b. cheese
    c. chicken salad
    d. canned foods

4. Viruses are food-related pathogens because they are _____.
    a. grown in foods that we eat
    b. easily killed when we cook foods
    c. easily spread by fecal-hand-oral route contamination of food
    d. only rarely responsible for causing illness

5. Which of the following could be a source of Shigella?

    a. Drinking water

    b. Potato salad

    c. Turkey

    d. Salmon fish filet

6. Preventing illness from parasites requires that all foods _____.

    a. are cooked to the customer's liking

    b. containing parasites are carefully looked at to ensure that no parasites are seen on the food

    c. are thoroughly washed to remove parasites from the food

    d. are purchased from approved sources

7. Keeping lunch meats past their use-by date increases the risk of which of the following foodborne illnesses?

    a. Shigellosis

    b. Listeriosis

    c. Yersiniosis

    d. Salmonellosis

8. Foodborne illnesses caused by viruses are mostly spread by each of the following except _____.

    a. when cooling foods

    b. contaminated water

    c. ill employees practicing poor hygiene

    d. individuals touching foods with their bare hands

9. Common symptoms of foodborne illness include _____.

    a. diarrhea, fever, and abdominal cramps

    b. diarrhea, fever, and leg cramps

    c. diarrhea, headache, and abdominal cramps

    d. diarrhea, headache, and leg cramps

10. Controlling for time and temperature is best for preventing _____.

    a. parasites

    b. viruses

    c. bacteria

    d. fungi

FDA Food Code References

Chapter 2 – Management

- 2-1 Supervision
    - 2-103.11 Person in Charge
- 2-2 Employee Health
    - 2-201.12 Exclusions and Restrictions
    - 2-201.13 Removal, Adjustment, or Retention of Exclusions and Restrictions

Annex 3 – Public Health Reasons/Administrative Guidelines

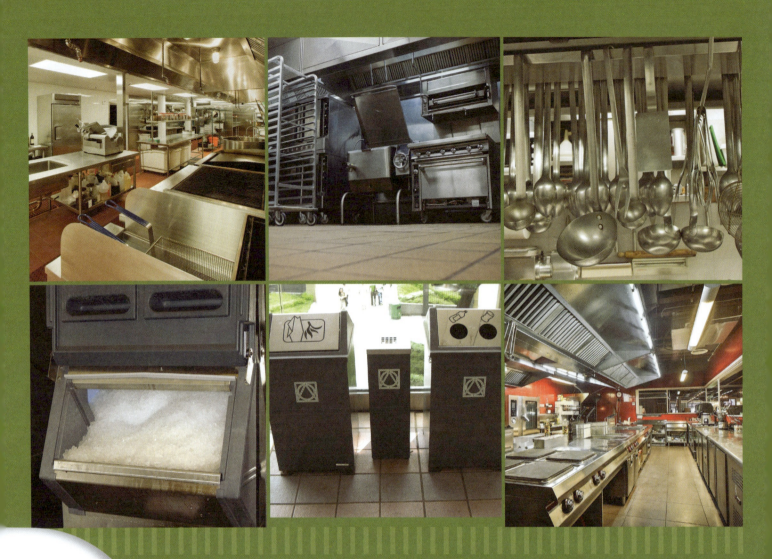

Chapter 4:
Core Food Safety Features

Chapter 4: Goals

In this chapter, participants will learn to:

- Identify core safety features of a food service and retail operation.
- Apply knowledge of core food safety features for expansion, renovation, or new food handling processes.
- Understand regulatory requirements involving building design, materials, space, equipment, and utility installations.
- Recognize sanitary features associated with different surfaces.
- Define backflow and the concern to food safety.

Chapter 4: Myth or Fact

(Check one.)

1. The person-in-charge is not responsible for the physical features in the food service or retail establishment.
   ✓ Myth ___ Fact

2. A broken light fixture will not be a problem during an inspection.
   ✓ Myth ___ Fact

3. Backflow prevention devices protect the water supply from an establishment's plumbing system.
   ___ Myth ✓ Fact

4. A food establishment can install carpet in food preparation areas when a cleaning program is in place.
   ✓ Myth ___ Fact

5. Ventilation systems keep operations free of excessive heat, steam, condensation, vapors, obnoxious odors, smoke, and fumes.
   ___ Myth ✓ Fact

Core Food Safety Features of a Food Service or Retail Establishment

A food service or retail premises must meet core food safety features. Core food safety features are the physical components of the establishment's premises related to:

- a safe water supply;
- plumbing system;
- sanitation and cleanliness;
- food equipment placement;
- food equipment cleaning;
- physical conditions;
- item storage; and
- facilities to ensure employee hygiene.

The PIC has to understand the impact that the physical condition and sanitation of the operation have on food safety. Many of the structural features of a food establishment are subject to requirements set by local regulatory authorities. The PIC has the responsibility of ensuring that food handling operations are conducted in a facility that is maintained in a safe and sanitary condition.

Regulatory requirements may involve:

- building design;
- materials;
- space allocations;
- equipment selection;
- utility installation; and
- cleanable finishes.

Different food products and processes impact the type of equipment, physical facility design, and maintenance needed in an operation. Food regulations may require a plan review in order to obtain approval for new construction, renovation, alteration, changes in menu, or changes in handling processes. During this time, the PIC must maintain control of the food service or retail establishment in order to avoid food safety risks.

Food Equipment and Utensils

Equipment manuals provide manufacturer guidelines for:

- equipment use and specification;
- personal protective equipment;
- approved lubricants;

- preventative maintenance requirements;
- maintenance tools; and
- cleaning supplies needed to properly maintain equipment.

The PIC must communicate and train staff to use equipment safely and properly. Food equipment and utensil use must not contribute to food contamination. To ensure food safety and prevent food contamination, equipment, and utensils must be:

- constructed with safe materials that will not transfer harmful chemicals to foods;
    - free of lead (pewter), copper, zinc (galvanized), etc.
- made with materials that are durable, corrosion-resistant, and nonabsorbent;
- resistant to distortion, deterioration, or decomposition;
- sufficient in weight and thickness to withstand repeated washing;
- finished with a smooth, easily cleanable surface that can be effectively cleaned and sanitized; and
- selected to meet proper usage and capacity.

 **Equipment**

Food equipment that is certified or classified for sanitation by an American National Standards Institute (ANSI)-accredited certification program is deemed to meet material, construction, design, accuracy, and functionality requirements as specified in the Food Code. Some symbols to look for on equipment are:

Equipment must be installed to allow for effective cleaning and pest control. Proper installation will prevent soil and moisture accumulation, the attraction of insects and rodents, and the growth of pathogens that can contaminate food. If equipment is not on casters for easy moving or is not light enough to be moved, then the equipment will need to be properly spaced or sealed. Equipment must be spaced at least 6 inches (15 cm) away from walls and other equipment.

Counter-mounted equipment installation:

- Sealed to the counter or elevated on legs that are at least 4 inches (10 cm) off of the counter.

Floor-mounted equipment installation:

- Sealed to the floor or elevated on legs that are at least 6 inches (15 cm) off of the floor.

Display shelving units, display refrigeration units, and display freezer units located in the consumer retail areas that are not often installed to make routine cleaning easy, require scheduled cleaning to maintain sanitary conditions. Equipment must be in good, working condition. Immediately stop using broken or defective equipment and contact the appropriate service provider for repairs.

Structural Components of the Establishment

Exterior and interior areas of the establishment need to meet economic, functional, safety, and regulatory requirements. The facility layout, space allocation, and material choices must also meet the sanitation and food handling safety needs of the operation.

Exterior Areas

Exterior building surfaces, including roofs, must be designed and constructed to prevent potential food contamination from:

- weather conditions;
- windblown dirt and debris; and
- insects, rodents, birds, or other pests.

The exterior surfaces and conditions must also not attract, harbor, or permit pest breeding. Pest control efforts associated with exterior conditions focus on waste storage areas to prevent attraction and openings into the building structure.

Exterior building openings, such as doors and windows, must be tight fitting when closed, or protected when opened with appropriate screening, entry devices, automatic closers, air curtains, or other means to prevent pest entry.

Garbage, refuse, recyclables, and returnables must be stored in areas that are constructed with materials that are nonabsorbent, durable, cleanable, and smooth. These areas must be able to withstand routine cleaning.

Interior Areas

All interior areas require proper construction and finishing that facilitate cleaning and sanitation requirements. Specific considerations apply to particular interior design features, surface material selection, and special requirements needed for particular aspects of the food operation. These considerations apply to uses or conditions that include:

- Carpet selection in non-food areas such as customer waiting or dining areas.
    - A planned maintenance program is required for carpeting.
- Anti-slip floor surface finishes provided for safety reasons.
    - These surfaces require additional maintenance and/or special cleaning methods.
- Acoustic tile suspended ceilings.
    - These must be selected for areas where they will not be subject to soiling, moisture, heat, or vapors.
- Utility lines and piping location and installation.
    - Placement must permit easy access and cleaning of surrounding surfaces.
- Utility lines including plumbing, electrical, and mechanical service connections need to be installed with penetration sleeves.
    - These penetration sleeves must be sealed in a durable, cleanable, and sanitary manner.

- Coving at floor and wall juncture.
    - When installed in dry areas, it cannot provide openings greater than 1/32 inch (1 mm), or when installed in areas subject to water flushing, it must be sealed.
- Floors subject to wet conditions or water flushing must be graded for cleaning.
    - Proper drainage prevents water pooling, insect or rodent attraction, and reduces problems with certain pathogens such as *Listeria monocytogenes* that grow in wet conditions.
- Wall and ceiling attachments such as light fixtures, ventilation system duct work, decorative items, signs and other similar fixtures.
    - These items must be constructed to be easily cleanable.
    - Decorative items for aesthetic or ambiance purposes not constructed of easily cleanable materials must be easily removed and replaced when soiled.
- Heating, ventilation, and air conditioning systems.
    - These systems require that the design and installation of the make-up air intake and exhaust vents do not cause contamination of food or food contact surfaces.

Interior Storage Areas

Storage locations must protect:

- Foods;
- Cleaned and sanitized equipment and utensils;
- Clean linens; and
- Single-service and single-use articles

from contamination hazards and **poisonous or toxic materials**.

Storage of these items cannot be located:

- In locker rooms;
- In toilet rooms;
- In garbage rooms;
- In mechanical rooms;
- Under sewer lines that are not shielded to intercept potential drips;
- Under leaking water lines including leaking automatic fire sprinkler heads or under lines on which water has condensed;
- Under open stairwells; and
- Under other sources of contamination.

Handwashing Facilities

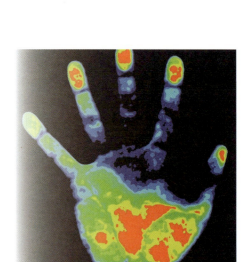

Handwashing sinks are a lavatory, a basin or vessel for washing, a wash basin, or a plumbing fixture especially placed for use in personal hygiene and designed for the washing of the hands. Every food operation must have at least one handwashing sink. The sinks must be conveniently located in areas near food preparation, warewashing, and toilet rooms.

Handwashing sinks must:

- Be accessible for use at all times.
- Be used only for handwashing.
- Have running water with adequate flow that is at least 100ºF (37.8ºC).
- Be stocked with soap.
- Have an effective means of drying hands:
    - Individual, disposable towels;
    - A continuous towel system that supplies the user with a clean towel;
    - A heated-air hand-drying device; or
    - A high air velocity hand-drying device.
- Have a waste receptacle for disposable towels.
- Have a sign or poster notifying employees to wash their hands.

Toilet Rooms

Sanitary toilet facilities prevent contamination from human waste. Waste can contain disease pathogens that could contaminate food by employees or pests. At least one toilet room with at least one toilet that is conveniently located for employee use is required for every food establishment. State and local laws may have additional mandates regarding the required numbers of toilet fixtures and urinals, separation of facilities, and patron accessibility. Minimum standards that apply to the toilet room include:

1. When located within the food operation premises, it must be enclosed and provided with a tight-fitting and self-closing door.

2. It must have:

    a. toilet tissue at each toilet.

    b. a covered receptacle for sanitary napkin disposal when the toilet room is used by females.

Service Sinks for Disposal of Liquid Cleaning Waste

Food service or retail operations require at least one service sink or one curbed cleaning station. They must be conveniently located and equipped with a floor drain. Service sinks are for cleaning mops or similar wet floor cleaning tools, and disposing of mop water.

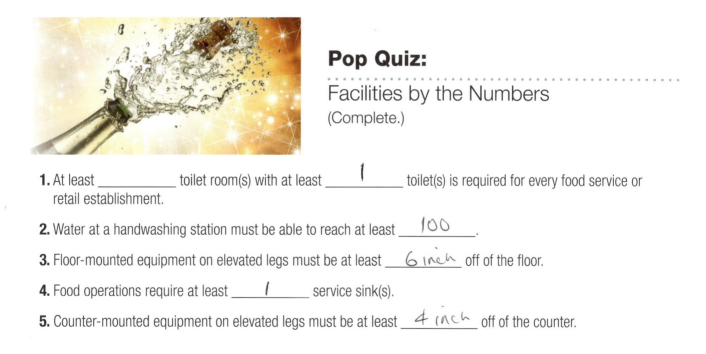

Pop Quiz:
Facilities by the Numbers
(Complete.)

1. At least _____ toilet room(s) with at least __1__ toilet(s) is required for every food service or retail establishment.

2. Water at a handwashing station must be able to reach at least __100__.

3. Floor-mounted equipment on elevated legs must be at least __6 inch__ off of the floor.

4. Food operations require at least __1__ service sink(s).

5. Counter-mounted equipment on elevated legs must be at least __4 inch__ off of the counter.

Lighting

Light fixtures must provide adequate lighting to accomplish food handling and facility maintenance tasks. Food areas must have light bulbs (or lamps) that are shielded, coated, or shatter-resistant. This protects food and food contact surfaces from glass due to bulb (or lamp) breakage. An infrared or heat lamp hot food display or holding unit should have a shield surround and extend beyond the bulb.

Food Code Minimum Lighting Levels

Food preparation task areas:
  50 foot candles (540 lux) at the work surface

General work areas and service areas:
  20 foot candles (215 lux) at a distance of 30 inches (75 cm) above the floor

Storage areas:
  10 foot candles (108 lux) at a distance of 30 inches (75 cm) above the floor

Ventilation System

Ventilation systems keep operations free of excessive heat, steam, condensation, vapors, obnoxious odors, smoke, and fumes. These systems must meet fire code specifications. Properly designed, installed, and operating ventilation systems will prevent hazards or nuisances from these conditions. Proper ventilation prevents accumulation of fats, oils, and similar wastes from soiling walls, ceilings, and other equipment. These systems need maintenance in order to prevent contamination of food and food contact surfaces. The PIC is responsible for:

- Routine and proper cleaning of the hoods and filters;
- Maintaining ducts and fire suppression system by contracting professional services;
- Protecting food and equipment from contamination during the cleaning and maintenance process;
- Proper placement of cooking equipment under hoods; and
- Ensuring proper ventilation throughout the facility.

Water Supply

The PIC is responsible for ensuring the safety of the water supply including proper temperature and water pressure requirements being used in the food establishment. Contaminated water can become a vehicle for carrying harmful chemicals or pathogens. Water used for drinking and food preparation is called **potable water**. Potable water must come from an approved source that meets federal and/or local regulatory requirements. Water used for food operations can be from a public water system supplied by a local municipality or from a regulated well or other nonpublic water system or source. Periodic testing is required for every water supply to ensure that it is safe and meets required standards. The PIC is responsible for ensuring that required water testing records are current when water is not being supplied directly from a regulated municipal water supply. When approved, a water supply source can include:

    a. An approved public water main;

    b. Nonpublic water main, water pumps, pipes, hoses, connections, and other components that make up the plumbing system;

    c. Water transport vehicles with enclosed water tanks;

    d. A supply of containers of commercially bottled drinking water;

e. One or more closed portable water containers;

f. An on-premises water storage tank; or

g. Piping, tubing, or hoses connected to an approved source that is located near the establishment.

Water Supply

Federal water quality standards are established by the U.S. Environmental Protection Agency (EPA). Food service and retail operators can contact their water supply authority for current water quality test results. When water is not supplied by a municipal water source, the water control authority in the state or local jurisdiction can be contacted to obtain water testing requirements.

Water Supply Protection

Plumbing systems must be designed and installed with approved materials and components to ensure the safety of the water supply. Plumbing system installation must prevent cross-connections and ensure that potable water is separate from non-potable liquid sources of contamination. Cross-connections allow for backflow of contaminates into the water system. **Backflow** can occur when negative pressure creates back siphonage, which causes contamination of the water system. Cross-connections and backflow situations can occur with:

- Ice machines;
- Dishwashers;
- Soda carbonators;
- Coffee makers; or
- Hoses attached to a water faucet with the other end submerged in a liquid.

Backflow prevention devices are often required to protect a potable water supply. A vacuum breaker can be installed to stop the reverse flow of the water. An air gap is the best protection against a cross-connection. An **air gap** is the physical separation of air between the water supply and plumbing equipment.

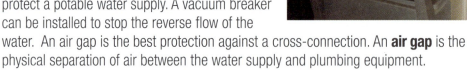

Sewage and liquid waste plumbing drainage systems, septic systems, and waste drainage plumbing fixtures including grease traps, and condensate drainage systems, that must be maintained in good repair and condition to ensure liquid wastes do not contaminate food or the food establishment premises.

Record Keeping

The PIC needs to be prepared to show to the regulatory authority the location of wells, septic systems, water treatment devices, and backflow prevention devices along with their associated records for inspection, testing, and service.

Waste and Recyclable Facilities and Equipment

The PIC must ensure that the handling and storing of waste and recyclables is done in a sanitary manner to minimize odors, prevent pests, and reduce the soiling of food preparation and food service areas. Maintaining waste receptacles and storage areas in a sanitary condition requires that:

- The location of designated indoor and outdoor storage areas be separate from food, food contact equipment, and utensils;
- Containers be constructed with material that is durable, nonabsorbent, leak proof, pest resistant, and cleanable;
- There are enough containers to hold the appropriate amount of waste;
- Large waste containers must have drain plugs installed;
- Returned items be discarded properly;
- Products held for composting and recycling be stored to avoid contamination;
- Fats, oils, and grease are stored in appropriate leak-proof containers; and
- Storage areas and containers be maintained and cleaned.

Pop Quiz:
Waste and Water
(Check one.)

1. An air gap is the physical link between the water supply and plumbing equipment.
___Yes ✓No

2. Plumbing systems must be designed and installed to ensure the safety of the water supply.
✓Yes ___No

3. Every food service or retail establishment must have both a men's and women's toilet room.
___Yes ✓No

4. A food operation that uses a toilet to dispose of mop waste water will not require installation of a service sink.
___Yes ✓No

5. Light fixtures in food areas must have light bulbs that are shielded, coated, or shatter-resistant.
✓Yes ___No

Chapter 4
Food Code Definitions

- **Food establishment:** an operation that

    (a) stores, prepares, packages, serves, vends food directly to the consumer, or otherwise provides food for human consumption such as a restaurant; satellite or catered feeding location; catering operation if the operation provides food directly to a consumer or to a conveyance used to transport people; market; vending location; conveyance used to transport people; institution; or food bank; and

    (b) relinquishes possession of food to a consumer directly, or indirectly through a delivery service such as home delivery of grocery orders or restaurant takeout orders, or delivery service that is provided by common carriers.

- **Handwashing sink:** a lavatory, a basin or vessel for washing, a wash basin, or a plumbing fixture especially placed for use in personal hygiene and designed for the washing of the hands. It also includes an automatic handwashing facility.

- **Poisonous or toxic materials:** substances that are not intended for ingestion and are grouped into four categories:
(1) Cleaners and sanitizers, which include cleaning and sanitizing agents and agents such as caustics, acids, drying agents, polishes, and other chemicals;
(2) Pesticides, except sanitizers, which include substances such as insecticides and rodenticides;
(3) Substances necessary for the operation and maintenance of the establishment such as nonfood-grade lubricants and personal care items that may be deleterious to health; and
(4) Substances that are not necessary for the operation and maintenance of the establishment and are on the premises for retail sale, such as petroleum products and paints.

- **Premises:**
(1) The physical facility, its contents, and the contiguous land or property under the control of the permit holder; or
(2) The physical facility, its contents, and the land or property not described in subparagraph (1) of this definition if its facilities and contents are under the control of the permit holder and may impact food establishment personnel, facilities, or operations, and a food establishment is only one component of a larger operation such as a health care facility, hotel, motel, school, recreational camp, or prison.

Chapter 4
Conclusion

A PIC must ensure that core food safety items are appropriate, correctly installed, and properly maintained. The facility must be maintained in a clean and safe condition to ensure that food is protected from contamination. A safe and clean facility is required in order to be able to serve and sell safe food.

Chapter 4

Check for Understanding
(Circle one.)

1. Waste storage containers must be constructed with materials that are _____.
    a. durable, absorbent, leak proof, pest resistant, and cleanable
    b. durable, nonabsorbent, leak proof, pest resistant, and cleanable
    c. flexible, nonabsorbent, leak proof, pest resistant, and cleanable
    d. flexible, absorbent, leak proof, pest resistant, and cleanable

2. Core food safety features include _____.
    a. needed facilities for employee hygiene
    b. good repair and condition of the facility
    c. safe water supply for the facility
    d. all of the above

3. Which of the following keeps operations free of excessive heat, steam, condensation, vapors, obnoxious odors, smoke, and fumes?
    a. Plumbing system
    b. Electrical system
    c. Ventilation system
    d. Mechanical system

4. When approved, a water supply source can include all except _____.
    a. an approved public water main
    b. water transport vehicles
    c. containers of rain water
    d. an on-premise water storage tank

5. Exterior doors or windows are properly protected except for the use of _____.
    a. cardboard
    b. air curtains
    c. automatic closures
    d. screens

6. The Food Code minimum lighting level for food preparation task areas is _____.
    a. 10 foot candles
    b. 20 foot candles
    c. 40 foot candles
    d. 50 foot candles

7. Food items can be stored with _____.

   a. cleaning chemicals

   b. employee's personal items

   c. clean linens

   d. cleaning utensils

8. Equipment must be sealed to tabletops and floor or be _____ from the tabletop and _____ from the floor.

   a. 4 inches (10 cm) and 10 inches (25 cm)

   b. 6 inches (15 cm) and 4 inches (10 cm)

   c. 4 inches (10 cm) and 6 inches (15 cm)

   d. 12 inches (30 cm) and 24 inches (60 cm)

9. A handwashing sink is required to have the following features except _____.

   a. hot running water

   b. soap for washing

   c. a waste receptacle for towel waste

   d. hand sanitizer

10. Light fixtures must be covered to prevent which contamination?

   a. Biological

   b. Chemical

   c. Physical

   d. Radiological

FDA Food Code References

Chapter 4 – Equipment, Utensils & Linens
- 4-4 Location and Installation
  - 4-401 Location
  - 4-401.11 Equipment, Clothes Washers and Dryers, and Storage Cabinets, Contamination Prevention
  - 4-402 Installation
  - 4-402.11 Fixed Equipment, Spacing or Sealing
  - 4-402.12 Fixed Equipment, Elevation or Sealing

Chapter 5 – Water, Plumbing & Waste
- 5-2 Plumbing System
  - 5-201 Materials
  - 5-202 Design, Construction, and Installation
  - 5-203 Numbers and Capacities
  - 5-204 Location and Placement
  - 5-205 Operation and Maintenance
- 5-5 Refuse, Recyclables, and Returnables
  - 5-501 Facilities on the Premises
  - 5-502 Removal
  - 5-503 Facilities for Disposal and Recycling

Chapter 6 – Physical Facilities
- 6-1 Materials for Construction and Repair
  - 6-101 Indoor Areas
  - 6-102 Outdoor Areas
- 6-2 Design, Construction, and Installation
  - 6-201 Cleanability
  - 6-202 Functionality
- 6-3 Numbers and Capacities
  - 6-301 Handwashing Sinks
  - 6-302 Toilets and Urinals
  - 6-303 Lighting
  - 6-304 Ventilation
  - 6-305 Dressing Areas and Lockers
  - 6-306 Service Sinks
- 6-5 Maintenance and Operation
  - 6-501 Premises, Structures, Attachments, and Fixtures - Methods

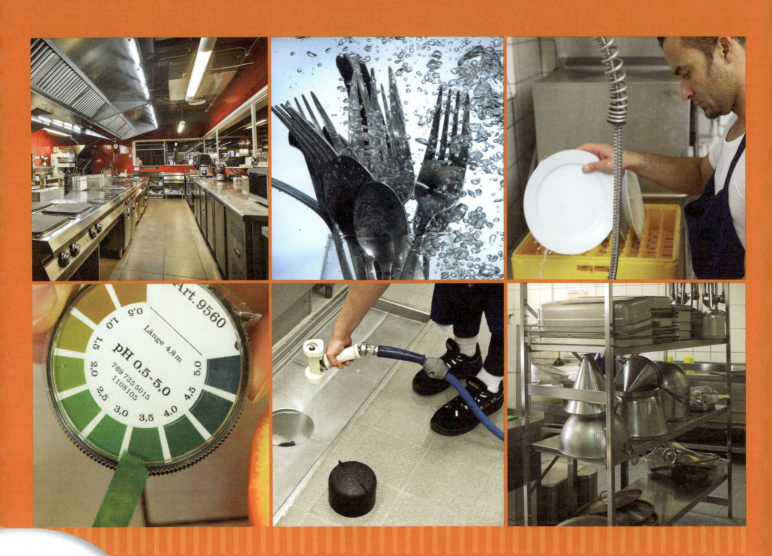

Chapter 5:
Preventing Contamination by Using Proper Cleaning, Sanitizing, and Pest Control

Chapter 5: Goals

In this chapter, participants will learn to:

- Define the difference between cleaning and sanitizing.
- Apply different cleaning methods.
- Identify factors that can influence the effectiveness of chemical sanitizers.
- Recognize the importance of chemical storage in preventing contamination.
- Understand how to apply effective pest control measures.

Chapter 5: Myth or Fact

(Check one.)

1. To prevent food contamination, food-contact surfaces of equipment in constant use need to be cleaned daily.
   ✓ Myth ___ Fact   every 4 hours

2. Cleaning is the process of removing dirt and other contaminates from a surface.
   ___ Myth ✓ Fact

3. The PIC is not responsible for ensuring that chemicals are safely stored, dispensed, used, and disposed of according to law.
   ✓ Myth ___ Fact

4. Equipment does not have to be cleaned if it is properly sanitized.
   ✓ Myth ___ Fact

5. Active managerial control includes focusing on preventing contamination of equipment and utensil surfaces.
   ___ Myth ✓ Fact

Cleaning and Sanitizing Overview

Using contaminated equipment is one of the CDC's five most common risk factors that cause foodborne illness. Food service and retail operations must be clean, and food-contact utensils and equipment must be properly cleaned and sanitized to keep food and customers safe. Conducting self-inspections enables the PIC to monitor cleaning and sanitizing effectiveness. Self-inspections can also identify risks to the operation. Preventing equipment contamination also involves having an effective pest control management program and proper storage of chemicals. The PIC must oversee procedures to ensure that chemicals are safely stored, dispensed, used, and disposed of according to the manufacturer's guidelines and the law. Also to prevent exposure to chemicals, persons conducting cleaning and sanitizing must use the appropriate personal protective equipment (PPE) such as gloves, goggles, and/or aprons.

Cleaning

Cleaning is the process used to remove dirt and other contaminates from a surface. All areas of the operation including walls, floors, ceilings, and equipment must be cleaned on a regular basis. There are many cleaners that can be used to clean different equipment surfaces and different types of dirt or soil. Examples of cleaners include:

- Detergents: used for everyday cleaning
- Degreasers: used to remove grease from equipment
- Delimers: used for hard water buildup
- Abrasive cleaners: used to remove stuck-on materials

Selection or use of a cleaner will depend upon three basic issues:

- The materials that are being cleaned
    - metal, glass, wood, tile, plastic, etc.
- The type of soil or dirt
    - heavy grease buildup, smudge marks, hard water buildup, etc.
- Type of contamination
    - biological, chemical, or physical

Cleaning Methods

Removing dirt or soil from surfaces requires different cleaners and methods. The following chart describes cleaning methods often used within food service or retail operations.

Cleaning Methods

Dry cleaning methods: brushing, scraping, vacuuming

Pre-cleaning methods: flushing, soaking, scrubbing with abrasives

Wet cleaning methods: manual or mechanical ways to apply cleaners or detergents
- This method includes the use of hot water, hoses, buckets, spray bottles, brushes, scouring pads, high-pressure sprays, or ultrasonic devices.

Loading methods: where and how items are positioned and placed to be cleaned in racks, baskets, or conveyors in a mechanical warewashing machine
- This method will affect the cleaning of these items and how thorough or effective the cleaning will be.

Rinsing methods: rinsing an item being cleaned matters, particularly when the cleaner can be a contaminant
- This method includes removal of cleaning abrasives or detergent-sanitizer solutions from a surface being cleaned.

The equipment used for cleaning must be cleaned at least daily or as frequently as needed to prevent contamination of the equipment and utensils being cleaned. Separate cleaning equipment is needed for food preparation areas, restrooms, and service areas.

Sanitizing

Sanitizing is the process used to reduce pathogens to safe levels on a clean surface. This can be done by using heat, chemicals, or other effective means.

Heat Sanitizing

Heat sanitizing requires raising the surface temperature of items being sanitized high enough to kill or reduce the number of pathogens to safe levels.

- Using hot water to sanitize in a three-compartment sink requires that the item being sanitized be immersed in hot water at least 171°F (77.2°C) for at least 30 seconds.
- Using hot water to sanitize in a warewashing machine usually requires that the hot water coming out of the water outlet manifold be at least 180°F (82.2°C) or 165°F (73.9°C) if in a stationary single-rack machine. Check manufacturer's specifications for detailed requirements.

Chemical Sanitizing

Chemical sanitizing relies on the use of chemicals at appropriate levels to kill pathogens. There are different chemicals that can be used when sanitizing; the most common chemical sanitizers include:

- Quaternary ammonium compounds (quats);
- Chlorine; and
- Iodine compounds.

It is important to always follow sanitizer label instructions when using chemicals. When testing the sanitizer concentration, use the appropriate sanitizer test strip or kit. If the chemical is too strong, it can cause a chemical contamination and be unsafe; if not strong enough, it will not be effective. The following chart provides basic information for common sanitizers and their use under different conditions.

Chemical	Concentration Range mg/L (ppm)	Water Hardness	Water pH	Minimum Temperature °F (°C)	Minimum Contact Time
Chlorine	25-49	N/A	pH of 10 or less	120°F (49°C)	10 seconds or as specified by the label
	50-99	N/A	pH of greater than 8 to 10	100°F (38°C)	7 seconds or as specified by the label
	50-99	N/A	pH of 8 or less	75°F (24°C)	7 seconds or as specified by the label
	100	N/A	pH of 10 or less	55°F (13°C)	10 seconds or as specified by the label
Iodine	12.5-25	N/A	pH of 5 or less or as specified by the label	68°F (20°C)	30 seconds or as specified by the label
Quats	Label direction	500 or less or as specified by the label	N/A	75°F (24°C)	30 seconds or as specified by the label

Both cleaning and sanitizing must be done to food-contact surfaces and equipment before use and at a minimum of every four hours when in constant use. The time frame could be less than four hours depending on how the food equipment or surface is being used and the foods being handled.

How to Clean and Sanitize

Establishments must develop Sanitation Standard Operating Procedures (SSOPs) and a master cleaning schedule in order to organize effectively for cleaning and sanitizing. These documents communicate when, how, what, and who will follow the procedures. There are five steps to cleaning and sanitizing. If any step is missed, the food-contact surfaces will not be safe.

1. Remove excessive food and dirt from the surface.
2. Wash the surface.
3. Rinse the surface.
4. Sanitize the surface.
5. Let the surface air dry.

While air drying and during storage, ensure that there is enough space for cleaned and sanitized equipment to protect from contamination.

When to Clean and Sanitize

Food-contact surfaces must be cleaned and sanitized at appropriate times to maintain their sanitary condition for safety during use. Cleaning and sanitizing is required:

- Every four hours during continual use when the food equipment or surface is not under temperature control.
    - Example: a cutting board at a food preparation station, or a slicer on a counter
- Every 24 hours when the food equipment or surface is maintained under temperature control.
    - Example: the insert pans for the hot or cold holding equipment
- After each use.
    - Example: a slicer used for one hour once a day
- Between different products, including major food allergens and different raw animal species with different cooking temperature requirements.
    - Example: cutting raw fish on a cutting board that will then be used to cut raw chicken
- Between raw and ready-to-eat product.
    - Example: tongs used to place raw ground beef on a grill that will then be used to remove the cooked ground beef from the grill
- Any time a task is interrupted and the surface may have been contaminated.
    - Example: when an employee leaves the preparation area to use the restroom

Cleaning Tools

The PIC must ensure that employees use the appropriate tools in the cleaning and sanitizing process.

- Use the proper tool for each designated task.
- Store tools in designated areas:
    - away from food; and
    - off of the floor.
- All tools must be clean and in good condition.

Wiping Cloths

Between proper cleaning and sanitizing, a wiping cloth may be used to remove food spills from a surface. A designated wiping cloth can be a:

- Single-use dry cloth;
- Paper towel;
- Wet reusable cloth stored in sanitizer solution;

- Cloth sprayed with a sanitizer solution; or
- A single-use disposable sanitizer wipe.

Proper use of these approved wiping clothes includes:

- Ensuring that the wiping cloths are kept clean and free of debris.
- Laundering or discarding them when needed.
- Avoiding cross-contamination with raw animal products and other items.
- Storing chemical sanitizing solutions away from food and food-contact surfaces.

Warewashing and Dishwashing Machines

Warewashing machines must be used in accordance with the manufacturer's instructions, and operated according to the machine's **data plate** (indicating the water pressure, wash, rinse, and sanitizing cycle times and temperatures). Warewashing machines can use hot water or chemicals for sanitization. The machine must be cleaned regularly and monitored to be sure it is:

a. Working correctly – all cycles meet the time and temperature requirements on the data plate.

b. Working effectively – items appear clean as expected, and sanitizer water temperature or chemical concentration meets specifications.

c. Maintained in good repair – all components are in working order and operate properly.

d. Calibrated – machines are regularly serviced, and a qualified technician ensures that temperature and sanitizer delivery system components are working correctly.

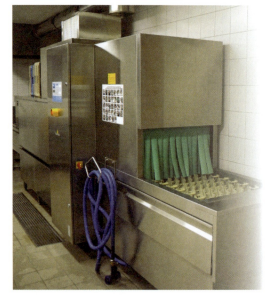

Utensils, dishes, flatware, and equipment washed in a warewashing machine must be pre-rinsed first, or scraped of any excess food residue and waste. This will keep the machine cleaner longer and prevent dirt or food from sticking to equipment and surfaces. Never overload the machine because it obstructs the cleaning and sanitizing process. After the items are cleaned, allow them to air dry upside down, or in an appropriate manner that permits drying and prevents contamination of food-contact surfaces.

Manual Warewashing and Dishwashing

When using a three-compartment sink, always clean the drain boards and sinks before starting the warewashing process. Fill sinks with the proper water, detergents, and sanitizers, and follow these steps:

1. Scrape extra food and dirt from dishes.

2. Wash the dishes.
- Use detergent and 110ºF (43.3ºC) water

3. Rinse the dishes.
   - In 110ºF (43.3ºC) water or using a spray nozzle
4. Sanitize the dishes.
   - Use appropriate chemical sanitizer levels or hot water temperatures
   - Use a clock to monitor contact time
5. Air dry utensils or equipment.
   - Dry upside down or in a position to drain off and dry food-contact surfaces.

Warewashing Water Temperatures

Check manual and mechanical warewashing water temperatures frequently. Keep the appropriate temperature measuring device readily available.

Storage of Clean Equipment, Utensils, and Tableware

Cleaned and sanitized items, as well as single-use items, must always be stored in locations and handled in a way that will prevent contamination. To prevent contamination, store:

- Items at least 6 inches (15 cm) off of the floor;
- All food containers including cups and bowls upside down;
- Flatware and serving utensils with handles facing up; and
- Exposed equipment or utensil food-contact surfaces must be covered until ready for use.

Pop Quiz:
Cleaning by the Numbers
(Complete.)

1. When manually washing dishes, water must be at least __110__ °.
2. Quat sanitizers must be at least __75__ °.
3. Equipment that is in constant use must be cleaned every __4__ hours.
4. Clean equipment must be stored __6__ off of the floor.
5. When heat sanitizing in a three-compartment sink, water must be at least __171__ °.

Pest Control

Pests can contaminate food and food-contact surfaces. The PIC is responsible for monitoring and maintaining the operation to make sure it is free of insects, rodents, or other pests. The PIC must also ensure that any pesticide used does not contaminate food or food-contact surfaces and create a foodborne illness risk. Pests can leave behind fecal matter, urine, hair, or other body parts or fluids and spread diseases as they walk around, land on, or feed on food or surfaces within a food operation. Common pests that can contaminate surfaces and spread disease-causing organisms are flies, cockroaches, and rodents.

- Flies breed in dead or rotting organic matter, animal feces, and garbage. Flies can spread disease because when they land on food and surfaces, they vomit and defecate, which causes contamination.

- Cockroaches like warm, dark, moist, and tight places such as cracks and crevices in equipment and building structure surfaces. Cockroaches are most active when it is dark and can produce a strong oily odor. Female cockroaches will leave behind egg casings that can still hatch even when the cockroaches are gone.

- Rodents (mice and rats) chew on items such as food, wires, boxes, and containers, which results in the contamination and destruction of food and materials. Signs of rodent presence can include droppings, dirt tracks along walls, and the gathering of nesting materials. Rodents also defecate and urinate as they move around, thereby contaminating surfaces.

Other pests in a food service or retail operation that can require pest control include stored grain insects and beetles, ants, spiders, birds, and other insects or animals that find a home in the operation. Food contaminated by pests must be discarded.

Having an effective pest management program in place will help prevent pests from entering an operation and eliminate pests that do enter. Integrated Pest Management (IPM) utilizes pest control measures that do not rely solely on chemicals or pesticides. IPM practices focus on ways to prevent insect survival and reproduction based on eliminating food and housing through comprehensive sanitation practices and controls. Pest prevention includes:

1. Preventing pests from entering the operation
- Inspect delivery vehicles and incoming shipments for signs of pests.
- Doors and windows must:
    - Be kept closed or self-closing; and
    - Have screens or air curtains.
- Fill in cracks and holes in walls, ceilings, floors, and roofs.
- Ensure that all drains have covers or grates securely in place.

2. Preventing pests from accessing food and shelter
- Clean spills immediately.
- Maintain plumbing system piping and fixtures in good repair.
- Use proper drain treatments and fly devices.
- Remove and store garbage and waste in appropriate containers away from the operation.
- Store exposed foods in sealed pest-proof containers.
- Follow first-in first-out (FIFO) storage procedures.
- Keep food and equipment 6 inches (15 cm) off of the floor.
- Keep the operation clean and in good repair.

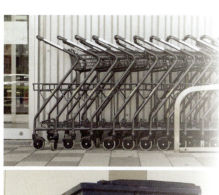

3. Working with a licensed pest control operator (PCO)
- A PCO should work with an establishment to develop preventative measures.
- Only use pesticides when the operation is closed. Protect food and food-contact surfaces and properly clean and sanitize surfaces that come in contact with pesticides.
- Manufactures guidelines for proper use, storage, and disposal for pesticides must be followed.
- Only a licensed PCO may apply pesticides.
- Ensure prompt removal of bird nests and dead pests.
- Locate and monitor insect-control devices, pest bait stations, glue boards, traps, and other control devices or materials to prevent contamination of surfaces and food.
- Use only non-toxic rodent-tracking powders.

Storage of Chemicals

Chemicals used, stored, or sold within the food operation, including cleaners, sanitizers, polishes, lubricants, pesticides, medicines, first-aid supplies or other personal care items can contaminate food or surfaces. When chemicals are stored improperly, chemical contamination can result, and people get sick or injured by unintended ingestion or contact. The following chart provides important chemical storage guidelines.

DO	DO NOT
Store chemicals away from food	Store chemicals above food
Store chemicals at least 6 inches (15cm) off of the floor	Store chemicals on the floor
Label all chemicals	Store chemicals in empty food containers

Material Safety Data Sheets

The Occupational Safety and Health Administration (OSHA) requires that employees have access to information about the chemicals to which they may be exposed. Material Safety Data Sheets (MSDS) provide this information. MSDS must be maintained for every chemical used and stored in the operation. Information about the chemical risks outlined in the MSDS must be accessible at all times to employees. The MSDS provides information about:

- Safe chemical use;
- Fire, explosion, and health hazards;
- Chemical characteristics; and
- First aid/emergency response.

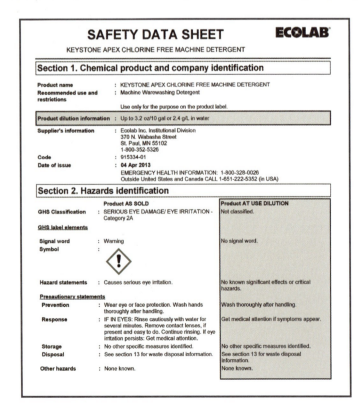

Pop Quiz:
Chemicals and Pests
(Check one.)

1. Chemicals can be stored above food storage areas.
   ___Yes ✓No

2. Chemical sanitizers are effective in all water temperatures.
   ___Yes ✓No

3. Cleaning does not have to be done if a sanitizer is used properly.
   ___Yes ✓No

4. Pests should have access to an operation.
   ___Yes ✓No

5. An MSDS is required for all chemicals used and stored in an operation.
   ✓Yes ___No

Chapter 5
Food Code Definitions

- **Food-contact surface:**
  (1) A surface of equipment or a utensil with which food normally comes into contact; or
  (2) a surface of equipment or a utensil from which food may drain, drip, or splash:
  (a) into a food, or
  (b) onto a surface normally in contact with food.

- **Poisonous or toxic materials:** substances that are not intended for ingestion and fall within four categories:
  (1) cleaners and sanitizers, which include cleaning and sanitizing agents and agents such as caustics, acids, drying agents, polishes, and other chemicals;
  (2) pesticides, except sanitizers, which include substances such as insecticides and rodenticides;
  (3) substances necessary for the operation and maintenance of the establishment such as nonfood-grade lubricants and personal care items that may be deleterious to health; and
  (4) substances that are not necessary for the operation and maintenance of the establishment and are on the premises for retail sale, such as petroleum products and paints.

- **Sanitization:** the application of cumulative heat or chemicals on cleaned food-contact surfaces that, when evaluated for efficacy, is sufficient to yield a reduction of 5 logs, which is equal to a 99.999% reduction, of representative disease microorganisms of public health importance.

- **Utensil:** a food-contact implement or container used in the storage, preparation, transportation, dispensing, sale, or service of food, such as kitchenware or tableware that is multiuse, single-service, or single-use; gloves used in contact with food; temperature-sensing probes of food temperature measuring devices; and probe-type price or identification tags used in contact with food.

- **Warewashing:** the cleaning and sanitizing of utensils and food-contact surfaces of equipment.

Chapter 5
Conclusion

Eliminating the risk of foodborne illness from contaminated equipment and utensils requires that the person-in-charge ensure that cleaning and sanitizing methods are being followed properly. Proper sanitation methods protect from contamination associated with chemicals, pests, and biological hazards.

Chapter 5

Check for Understanding
(Circle one.)

1. The proper sequence of steps to ensure effective cleaning and sanitizing is _____.
- **a.** wash, rinse, and sanitize
- **b.** rinse, wash, sanitize, and air dry
- **c.** remove dirt, wash, rinse, sanitize, and air dry
- **d.** remove dirt, rinse, sanitize, wash, and air dry

2. Which cleaner is best for everyday cleaning?
- **a.** Degreaser
- **b.** Detergent
- **c.** Abrasive cleaner
- **d.** Delimer

3. The Occupational Safety and Health Administration (OSHA) requires that employees have access to information about the chemicals they may be exposed to, which is provided in _____.
- **a.** the FDA Food Code
- **b.** the Material Safety Data Sheet (MSDS)
- **c.** a pest control operator (PCO)
- **d.** a cookbook

4. Pest control measures include all of the following except _____.
- **a.** preventing pests from entering the operation
- **b.** working with a licensed pest control operator (PCO)
- **c.** preventing pests from accessing food and shelter
- **d.** working with a food employee to spray pesticides

5. After cleaning, mops and brooms must be stored _____.
- **a.** on the floor, with food products
- **b.** off of the floor, with food products
- **c.** off of the floor, away from food products
- **d.** on the floor, away from food products

6. Wiping cloths are permitted for use to _____.
- **a.** clean and sanitize tabletops if stored in a sanitizing solution
- **b.** wipe off food preparation cutting boards if they are wet and maintained on the cutting board
- **c.** clean food spills if they are dry and clean
- **d.** keep hands clean while preparing sandwiches at the preparation table

7. Food surfaces are required to be cleaned and sanitized every four hours when _____.

    a. being stored in a deli case

    b. not being kept at hot or cold temperatures

    c. being used for dry spice products

    d. not in use

8. Warewashing machines can use hot water or chemicals to sanitize. Effective cleaning and sanitizing will only be accomplished when _____.

    a. hot water being used is at least 100ºF (37.8ºC)

    b. sanitizer is used before detergent

    c. machines are overloaded with dishes

    d. the machine is operating in accordance with the data plate specifications

9. Integrated Pest Management (IPM) practices ensure that chemical pesticides are _____.

    a. only used

    b. not used

    c. used when sanitation efforts fail

    d. used with sanitation efforts to control pests

10. Cups and bowls should be stored _____.

    a. on the floor

    b. against the wall

    c. upside down

    d. right-side up

FDA Food Code References

Chapter 4 – Equipment, Utensils & Linens
- 4-2 Design and Construction
    - 4-203.13 Pressure Measuring Devices, Mechanical Warewashing Equipment
    - 4-204.113 Warewashing Machine, Data Plate Operating Specifications
    - 4-204.114 Warewashing Machines, Internal Baffles
    - 4-204.115 Warewashing Machines, Temperature Measuring Devices
    - 4-204.116 Manual Warewashing Equipment, Heaters and Baskets
    - 4-204.117 Warewashing Machines, Automatic Dispensing of Detergents and Sanitizers
    - 4-204.118 Warewashing Machines, Flow Pressure Device
    - 4-204.119 Warewashing Sinks and Drainboards, Self-Draining
    - 4-204.120 Equipment Compartments, Drainage
- 4-3 Numbers and Capacities
    - 4-301.12 Manual Warewashing, Sink Compartment Requirements
    - 4-301.13 Drainboards
    - 4-302.13 Temperature Measuring Devices, Manual Warewashing
    - 4-302.14 Sanitizing Solutions, Testing Devices
- 4-5 Maintenance and Operation
    - 4-501.110 Mechanical Warewashing Equipment, Wash Solution Temperature
    - 4-501.111 Manual Warewashing Equipment, Hot Water Sanitization Temperatures

- 4-501.112 Mechanical Warewashing Equipment, Hot Water Sanitization Temperatures
- 4-501.113 Mechanical Warewashing Equipment, Sanitization Pressure
- 4-501.114 Manual and Mechanical Warewashing Equipment, Chemical Sanitization – Temperature, pH, Concentration, and Hardness
- 4-501.115 Manual Warewashing Equipment, Chemical Sanitization Using Detergent-Sanitizers
- 4-501.116 Warewashing Equipment, Determining Chemical Sanitizer Concentration
- 4-501.14 Warewashing Equipment, Cleaning Frequency
- 4-501.15 Warewashing Machines, Manufacturers' Operating Instructions
- 4-501.16 Warewashing Sinks, Use Limitation
- 4-501.17 Warewashing Equipment, Cleaning Agents
- 4-501.18 Warewashing Equipment, Clean Solutions
- 4-501.19 Manual Warewashing Equipment, Wash Solution Temperature
- 4-502 Utensils and Temperature and Pressure Measuring Devices
- 4-502.11 Good Repair and Calibration

- 4-6 Cleaning of Equipment and Utensils
    - 4-601.11 Equipment, Food-Contact Surfaces, Nonfood-Contact Surfaces, and Utensils
    - 4-602.11 Equipment Food-Contact Surfaces and Utensils
    - 4-602.12 Cooking and Baking Equipment
    - 4-602.13 Nonfood-Contact Surfaces
    - 4-603.11 Dry Cleaning
    - 4-603.12 Precleaning
    - 4-603.13 Loading of Soiled Items, Warewashing Machines
    - 4-603.14 Wet Cleaning
    - 4-603.15 Washing, Procedures for Alternative Manual Warewashing Equipment
    - 4-603.16 Rinsing Procedures
    - 4-603.17 Returnables, Cleaning for Refilling

- 4-7 Sanitization of Equipment and Utensils
    - 4-701.10 Food-Contact Surfaces and Utensils
    - 4-702.11 Before Use After Cleaning
    - 4-703.11 Hot Water and Chemical

- 4-9 Protection of Clean Items
    - 4-901 Drying
    - 4-901.11 Equipment and Utensils, Air-Drying Required
    - 4-901.12 Wiping Cloths, Air-Drying Locations
    - 4-902 Lubricating and Reassembling
    - 4-902.11 Food-Contact Surfaces
    - 4-902.12 Equipment
    - 4-903 Storing Contamination
    - 4-903.11 Equipment, Utensils, Linens, and Single-Service and Single-Use Articles
    - 4-903.12 Prohibitions
    - 4-904 Preventing Contamination
    - 4-904.11 Kitchenware and Tableware
    - 4-904.12 Soiled and Clean Tableware
    - 4-904.13 Preset Tableware
    - 4-904.14 Rinsing Equipment and Utensils after Cleaning and Sanitizing

Chapter 6 – Physical Facilities
- 6-5 Maintenance and Operation
    - 6-501.111 Controlling Pests
    - 6-501.112 Removing Dead or Trapped Birds, Insects, Rodents, and Other Pests

Chapter 7 – Poisonous or Toxic Materials
- 7-1 Labeling and Identification
    - 7-101 Original Containers
    - 7-102 Working Containers
- 7-2 Operational Supplies and Applications
    - 7-201 Storage
    - 7-202 Presence and Use
    - 7-202.12 Conditions of Use
    - 7-203 Container Prohibitions
    - 7-204 Chemicals
    - 7-205 Lubricants
    - 7-206 Pesticides
    - 7-206.11 Restricted Use Pesticides, Criteria
    - 7-206.12 Rodent Bait Stations
    - 7-206.13 Tracking Powders, Pest Control and Monitoring
    - 7-207 Medicines
    - 7-208 First Aid Supplies
    - 7-209 Other Personal Care Items
- 7-3 Stock and Retail Sale
    - 7-301 Storage and Display
    - 7-301 Storage and Display
    - 7-301.11 Separation

Chapter 6:
Applying Proper Personal Hygiene at Food Service and Retail Establishments

Chapter 6: Goals

In this chapter, participants will learn to:

- Identify good personal hygiene practices.
- Recognize management's role in employee health management.
- Identify proper work attire.
- Apply proper handwashing procedures, hand care, glove use, and hand antiseptic use.
- Be aware of procedures needed for responding to contamination events.

Chapter 6: Myth or Fact

(Check one.)

1. A conditional employee is the individual present at a food establishment responsible for the operation at the time of inspection.
✓ Myth ___ Fact

2. Medical alert bracelets cannot be worn around a food handler's wrist.
___ Myth ✓ Fact

3. Hand antiseptics (hand sanitizers) can be used instead of handwashing.
✓ Myth ___ Fact

4. First aid and other personal care items must be treated like any other hazardous chemicals.
___ Myth ✓ Fact

5. When food handlers are sick or have been recently exposed to certain illnesses or symptoms, they are not at risk for spreading pathogens to food and to customers.
✓ Myth ___ Fact

Proper Personal Hygiene Practices

Practicing poor personal hygiene is one of the five most common risk factors to food safety according to the Centers for Disease Control and Prevention (CDC). Food employees, conditional employees, and persons-in-charge can each potentially be a source of a foodborne illness. Good personal hygiene practices are required of all employees in order to prevent food contamination from biological, chemical, or physical hazards. Appropriate procedures must be implemented, followed, monitored, and maintained to ensure that food contamination does not occur or result from poor personal hygiene. Good personal hygiene practices serve to protect food and customer safety and prevent foodborne illness.

Work Attire

Personal hygiene controls include the following:

- Clothing
    - All employees must work in clean clothing.
- Aprons
    - Aprons can protect food from contamination that may be on clothing.
    - Aprons should only be worn in food preparation areas, and never when cleaning or taking out garbage.
    - Aprons must be kept clean.
    - Aprons cannot be worn into a restroom.
- Hair restraints
    - Hair must be pulled back and covered with a hat or hair net.
    - Beard restraints must also be worn.
- Jewelry
    - Only a plain metal band ring (such as a wedding ring) may be worn.
    - No bracelets or watches can be worn.
    - Medical alert bracelets cannot be worn around a food handler's wrist. It may be allowed around the ankle or as a necklace. When necklaces are worn for medical reasons, it is best to keep them tucked into the shirt.

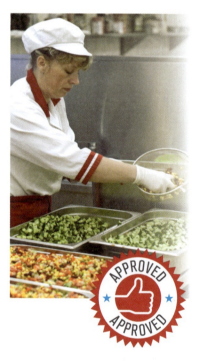

Washing Hands

Contaminated hands and skin are a source of fecal-hand-oral pathogens. Hands can also be a source of *Staphylococcus aureus* bacteria that can contaminate food. Hands, arms, and prosthetic devices must be kept clean. Proper handwashing is needed in order to prevent pathogens from transferring from a food handler to food or food-contact surfaces. Hands must be washed:

- Before and after handling raw product;
- Before putting on gloves to begin food-handling tasks;

- After using the restroom;
- After blowing nose/using a tissue;
- After touching hair, face, or body;
- After smoking, eating, or drinking;
- After handling chemicals;
- After handling money;
- After handling dirty equipment or utensils;
- Before returning to the food preparation area; and/or
- After any other activity that may contaminate hands.

It is important to wash hands properly in a handwashing sink or use approved automatic handwashing equipment. If not done correctly, contamination will remain on hands. Proper handwashing requires **at least 20 seconds** using hand soap or a cleaning compound and the following steps:

1. Wet hands and arms with running water that is at least 100ºF (37.7ºC);
2. Apply soap;
3. Scrub for 10-15 seconds between fingers, down wrists, palms, back of hands, and fingernails;
4. Rinse; and
5. Dry (clean disposable towel, heated-air hand dryer, or other approved means).

Avoid recontamination by using disposable paper towels or a similar clean barrier when touching surfaces such as faucet handles or the restroom door.

SURE Tip: Fingernail brushes, if used properly, can be effective tools in decontaminating under fingernails.

Hand Antiseptics

Hand antiseptics (hand sanitizers) can only be used in addition to handwashing. Never substitute the use of sanitizers or hand antiseptics for handwashing. Hand antiseptics only reduce pathogens on hands. They do not remove dirt from hands.

Gloves

Gloves are utensils. They must be in good repair and maintained in clean sanitary condition. Glove types include:

- **Single-use disposable gloves** – This type of glove can come in different styles, colors, and materials. To avoid latex allergic reactions, select gloves that are not made with natural rubber latex.
- **Multi-use gloves** – This type of glove must be washed, rinsed, and sanitized between tasks.
- **Cloth gloves or gloves made of readily cleanable materials** – These types of gloves are often slash-resistant in order to protect worker hands from cuts when working with knives or machinery. These types of gloves can only be used to handle food that is going to be cooked, and can be laundered to keep them clean.

Gloves are worn when handling ready-to-eat foods to prevent bare-hand contact. Other utensils, such as serving utensils (spoons, scoops, spatulas, etc.) and single-use tissue or paper (deli paper) can also be used. Always wash hands before putting on gloves to begin food-handling tasks. Make sure the gloves fit properly, are easily accessible, and are safe for food handling. Gloves must be changed when:

- switching tasks;
- changing products;
- dirty; or
- ripped.

SURE Tip: Food contamination from improper glove use, hand hygiene, or food handling will require corrective action. The PIC must ensure that the contaminated food is discarded and the employees are retrained on hygiene practices and procedures.

Hand Care

Along with having clean hands and wearing gloves, there are a few other things to consider for hand care.

- Fingernails must be kept short and clean. A food handler with long, painted, or fake fingernails poses a risk to food safety.
    - When approved, if something is applied to fingernails, gloves must be worn to prevent contamination of the food.
- Hand wounds must be covered with a bandage and a glove or finger cot.
- Open wounds on other parts of the body must also be covered with a bandage and waterproof cover.

Smoking, Eating, and Drinking

Food handlers cannot eat, smoke, or drink around food or food-contact surfaces. When this practice is not followed, pathogens can be transferred from the food handler to the food and cause contamination. Use designated areas away from preparation areas and food-contact surfaces to smoke, chew tobacco, eat, chew gum, or drink. Be sure to wash hands after doing these things and before returning to the food preparation area. Some operations are permitted to allow employees to drink fluids while working. They must use closed beverage containers so that no contamination will occur.

Tasting Food

There may be times when food needs to be sampled to make sure that it tastes as desired. When doing this, it is important to do it safely. Follow the steps below in order to sample food properly:

1. Place the food being tasted into a separate container.
2. Use a designated utensil to taste the item.
3. Taste the food away from the preparation area.
4. Throw away or wash the container and utensil.
5. Wash hands before returning to the food preparation area.

Pop Quiz:

Handwashing
(Check all that apply.)
N/A - not applicable

Hands must be washed:

1. ___Before ✓After ___N/A touching hair, face, or body
2. ✓Before ___After ___N/A returning to the food preparation area
3. ___Before ✓After ___N/A handling dirty equipment or utensils
4. ___Before ✓After ___N/A handling a pen
5. ___Before ✓After ___N/A handling the telephone
6. ✓Before ✓After ___N/A washing vegetables
7. ✓Before ✓After ___N/A handling raw product
8. ✓Before ___After ___N/A putting on gloves
9. ___Before ✓After ___N/A using the restroom
10. ___Before ✓After ___N/A blowing nose and using a tissue
11. ___Before ✓After ___N/A smoking, eating, or drinking
12. ___Before ✓After ___N/A handling chemicals
13. ___Before ✓After ___N/A handling money
14. ✓Before ___After ___N/A returning to the kitchen
15. ___Before ✓After ___N/A putting on a hairnet or beard guard

Employee Accommodations

Suitable facilities for employees' personal clothing, belongings, and uniforms need to be provided. These facilities must be in a designated room or area and kept in a clean, sanitary condition. This protects food, food employees, and work areas from contamination. The PIC should monitor food preparation and storage areas for the improper storage of personal items.

First Aid and Other Personal Care Items

Personal care items are used to maintain or enhance a person's health, hygiene, or appearance such as medicines, first-aid supplies, cosmetics, and toiletries. These items or substances may be poisonous, toxic, or a source of contamination.

First-aid and personal care items must be treated like hazardous chemicals in order to prevent accidental contamination. This can be done by:

- Using these items at different times than when food is being handled;
- Storing these items away from foods;
- Segregating these items when near food or stored with foods as in a refrigerator, so they cannot fall or leak into foods;
- Storing these items in leak-proof containers; and
- Labeling these items so that they cannot be confused with or mistaken for food or a food ingredient.

Employee Health Management and Reportable Health Illnesses

Food employees, conditional employees, and the PIC must be aware of their responsibility to report certain disease conditions and symptoms. The PIC must be notified by food employees of certain health conditions and must restrict or exclude food employees from working with food, based upon disease symptoms or illness. To **restrict** is to limit the activities of a food employee so that there is no risk of transmitting a disease that is transmissible through food, and so that the food employee does not work with exposed food, clean equipment, utensils, linens, or unwrapped single-service or single-use articles. To **exclude** means to prevent a person from entering or working as an employee in a food establishment.

Americans with Disabilities Act

Conditions that impact food safety do not fall under the protection of the Americans with Disabilities Act (ADA). Employees must report the diseases and symptoms that are listed below.

When a food handler is sick or has been recently exposed to a certain illness or disease symptom, they can spread pathogens to the food and customers. It is important and necessary at times to exclude food handlers from working in the food operation or restrict food handlers from handling food items in order to protect the food, the customers, and employees. Exclusions and restrictions will apply for the following conditions:

- When a food handler has a sore throat with fever: *Restrict*
    - He/she cannot work with food.
    - He/she cannot work at an operation that serves primarily highly susceptible populations. *Exclude*
- When a food handler has jaundice, vomiting, diarrhea, uncovered open wounds or lesions: *Exclude*
    - He/she cannot be at work.
    - He/she must report jaundice symptoms to the regulatory authority.
- When a food handler is diagnosed with one of the "Big 6" diseases, which are: *Excluded/Reported to health Authorities*
    - **H**epatitis A;
    - **E**. coli shiga toxin-producing;
    - **N**orovirus;
    - **S**higella;
    - **S**almonella typhi; and
    - **S**almonella nontyphoidal.
    - He/she cannot be at work.
    - He/she must be reported to the PIC and health department.

The "Big 6" is easily remembered with the acronym **"HENSSS."**

Following exclusion or restriction, the food handler can only return to work and normal duties when the conditions listed below are met, as needed, for a specific illness or symptom:

- Treatment is completed and effective.
- Clearance or permission is given by a health care practitioner.
- Illness symptoms or conditions are no longer communicable.

Employees infectious with a sore throat with fever, vomiting, or diarrhea must be symptom free for 24 hours prior to returning to work. Employees experiencing persistent sneezing, coughing, or a runny nose are required to be assigned to duties that minimize the potential risk of contaminating food and food-contact surfaces.

The following charts from the Food Code will provide helpful information and guidance to fulfill responsibilities in managing employee health conditions.

Key
- **D** = Diarrhea
- **F** = Fever
- **V** = Vomiting
- **J** = Jaundice
- **S** = Sore throat with fever

List I. Pathogens often transmitted by food which has been contaminated by infected persons who handled the food.

	D	F	V	J	S
1. Noroviruses	D	F	V		
2. Hepatitis A virus		F		J	
3. *Salmonella typhi* (typhoid-like fever)		F			
4. *Shigella* species	D	F	V		
5. *Staphylococcus aureus*	D		V		
6. *Streptococcus pyogenes*		F			S

List II. Pathogens occasionally transmitted by food which has been contaminated by infected persons who handled the food, but usually transmitted by a contaminated source or in food processing or by non-foodborne routes.

	D	F	V	J	S
1. *Campylobacter jejuni*	D	F	V		
2. *Cryptosporidium parvum*	D				
3. Shiga toxin-producing *Escherichia coli*	D		V		
4. *Giardia lamblia*	D				
5. Nontyphoidal *salmonella*	D	F	V		
6. *Vibrio cholerae* 01	D		V		
7. *Yersinia enterocolitica*	D	F	V		

Exclude or Restrict Decision Tree

When to Exclude or Restrict a Food Employee Who Reports a Symptom and When to Exclude a Food Employee Who Reports a Diagnosis with Symptoms Under the Food Code

Key

Listed Symptoms for Reporting
- **D** = Diarrhea
- **J** = Jaundice
- **ST with F** = Sore throat with fever
- **V** = Vomiting

- **HSP** = Highly susceptible population
- **Gen. Pop.** = General population
- **STEC** = Shiga toxin-producing Escherichia coli
- **NTS** = Nontyphoidal Salmonella

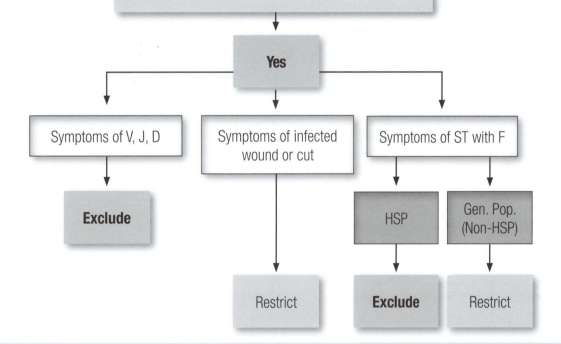

Is the Food Employee reporting listed symptoms? → Yes

- Symptoms of V, J, D → **Exclude**
- Symptoms of infected wound or cut → **Restrict**
- Symptoms of ST with F:
  - HSP → **Exclude**
  - Gen. Pop. (Non-HSP) → **Restrict**

If reporting a diagnosis with Hepatitis A, STEC, Norovirus, Salmonella typhi, NTS, Shigella, or symptoms of V or D

Exclude

Procedures for Responding to Contamination Events

Norovirus is responsible for greater than 50% of all foodborne gastroenteritis outbreaks. It is highly contagious, causes severe projectile vomiting and explosive diarrhea. High amounts of Norovirus are contained in these materials, which can cause the virus to spread onto environmental surfaces by direct and airborne contamination.

Stringent procedures on how to clean and disinfect vomit or fecal matter on contaminated surfaces are needed. These procedures need to include:

- Containment and segregation of contaminated areas to prevent exposure to others;
- How to handle ill individuals and how to assist individuals off of the premises;
- Training on how to clean, sanitize, and disinfect discharges and contaminated surfaces;
- Training on the proper use of required chemicals, equipment, and cleaning tools;
- Disposal of food that may have been contaminated;
- Disposal and/or cleaning and disinfection of tools and equipment used to clean up vomit or fecal matter;
- Training on and use of personal protective equipment for cleaning and disinfecting contaminated areas;
- Conditions under which the plan will be implemented; and
- When to use these procedures.

Pop Quiz:

Employee Health
(Check all that apply.)

Employees must be restricted and/or excluded if they have the following symptoms:

1. ✓ Hives
2. ✓ Vomiting
3. ___ Hiccups
4. ___ Coughing
5. ✓ Sore throat with fever
6. ___ Constipation
7. ___ Sneezing
8. ✓ Diarrhea
9. ___ Runny nose
10. ✓ Jaundice

Chapter 6
Food Code Definitions

- **Conditional employee:** a potential food employee to whom a job offer is made, conditional on responses to subsequent medical questions or examinations designed to identify potential food employees who may be suffering from a disease that can be transmitted through food and done in compliance with Title 1 of the Americans with Disabilities Act of 1990.

- **Employee:** the permit holder, person-in-charge, food employee, person having supervisory or management duties, person on the payroll, family member, volunteer, person performing work under contractual agreement, or other person working in a food establishment.

- **Exclude:** to prevent a person from entering or working as an employee in a food establishment.

- **Food Employee:** an individual working with unpackaged food, food equipment or utensils, or food-contact surfaces.

- **Personal care items:** items or substances that may be poisonous, toxic, or a source of contamination and are used to maintain or enhance a person's health, hygiene, or appearance. These include items such as medicines, first-aid supplies, and other items such as cosmetics, and toiletries such as toothpaste and mouthwash.

- **Person-in-charge (PIC):** the individual present at a food establishment who is responsible for the operation at the time of inspection.

- **Restrict:** to limit the activities of a food employee so that there is no risk of transmitting a disease that is transmissible through food and so that the food employee does not work with exposed food, clean equipment, utensils, linens, or unwrapped single-service or single-use articles.

Chapter 6
Conclusion

The CDC identified that practicing poor personal hygiene is one of the five most common risk factors to food safety. Chapter 6 focused on the behaviors of employees and management. Employees, conditional employees, and persons-in-charge each have important roles and critical responsibilities related to proper work attire and personal hygiene in order to prevent cross-contamination. To operate a safe business, it is essential to manage employee health, correctly respond to contamination events, apply personal hygiene practices, have proper hand care, and use gloves and hand antiseptics correctly.

Chapter 6

Check for Understanding
(Circle one.)

1. Which of the following can be worn by a food handler?
    a. Plain metal band ring
    b. Fake fingernails
    c. Unwashed apron
    d. Watch

2. The CDC identified that practicing poor personal hygiene is_____.
    a. not one of the five most common risk factors to food safety
    b. one of the five most common risk factors to food safety
    c. not as important as reheating food
    d. optional for employees and management

3. What can be done to prevent accidental contamination of food from first-aid and personal care items that are considered hazardous chemicals?
    a. Label these items so that they cannot be confused with or mistaken for food or a food ingredient.
    b. Locate or segregate these items when near food or stored with foods as in a refrigerator, so that they cannot fall or leak into foods.
    c. Store these items in leak-proof containers.
    d. All of the above.

4. In a food service or retail establishment, who must be aware of their responsibility to report certain disease conditions and symptoms?
    a. Food employees, conditional employees, and the PIC
    b. Food employees and conditional employees only
    c. Food employees and the PIC only
    d. The PIC only

5. Food handlers cannot _____ around food or food-contact surfaces.
    a. eat or smoke
    b. smoke or drink
    c. eat, smoke, or drink with an open container
    d. none of the above

6. Contaminated hands and skin are a source of _____.

    a. fecal-hand-oral pathogens

    b. *Staphylococcus aureus* bacteria

    c. a and b

    d. none of the above

7. Aprons can be worn when _____.

    a. taking out garbage

    b. in the restroom

    c. cleaning the dining room

    d. in the food preparation area

8. Which of the following is not a step in proper handwashing?

    a. Wetting hands and arms with running water at least 100ºF (37.7ºC)

    b. Applying hand antiseptics

    c. Rinsing

    d. Scrubbing for 10-15 seconds

9. Gloves must be worn when _____.

    a. clearing tables

    b. handling ready-to-eat foods

    c. handling utensils

    d. using the restroom

10. Good personal hygiene practices are required of all employees in order to prevent _____.

    a. biological hazards

    b. chemical hazards

    c. physical hazards

    d. biological, chemical, and physical hazards

FDA Food Code References

Chapter 2 – Management & Personnel

- 2-2 Employee Health
    - 2-201.11 Responsibility of Permit Holder, Person in Charge, and Conditional Employees
    - 2-201.12 Exclusions and Restrictions
    - 2-201.13 Removal, Adjustment, or Retention of Exclusions and Restrictions
- 2-3 Personal Cleanliness
    - 2-301 Hands and Arms
    - 2-301.11 Clean Condition
    - 2-301.12 Cleaning Procedure
    - 2-301.13 Special Handwash Procedures
    - 2-301.14 When to Wash
    - 2-301.15 Where to Wash
    - 2-301.16 Hand Antiseptics
    - 2-302 Fingernails
    - 2-302.11 Maintenance
    - 2-303 Jewelry
    - 2-303.11 Prohibition
    - 2-304 Outer Clothing
    - 2-304.11 Clean Condition
- 2-4 Hygienic Practices

- o 2-401 Food Contamination Prevention
- o 2-401.11 Eating, Drinking, or Using Tobacco
- o 2-401.12 Discharges from the Eyes, Nose, and Mouth
- o 2-402 Hair Restraints

Chapter 3 – Food

- 3-3 Protection From Contamination After Receiving
  - o 3-301.12 Preventing Contamination When Tasting

Chapter 6 – Physical Facilities

- 6-3 Numbers and Capacities
  - o 6-305.11 Designation (Dressing Areas and Lockers)
- 6-4 Location and Placement
  - o 6-403.11 Designated Areas (Employee Accommodations)
- 6-5 Maintenance and Operation
  - o 6-501.110 Using Dressing Rooms and Lockers (Employee Accommodations)

Chapter 7: Purchasing Food from Safe Sources

Chapter 7: Goals

In this chapter, participants will learn to:

- Define an approved source.
- Understand food standards and labeling.
- Identify reasons for rejecting food shipments.
- Recognize important food safety issues with specific foods.
- Apply safe food-handling practices to receiving, storing, and preparing food.

Chapter 7: Myth or Fact

(Check one.)

1. A food can be stored without concern for safety as long as strict temperature controls are maintained.
　✓ Myth ___ Fact

2. A food product coming from a known vendor is safe and will not need inspection when being received.
　✓ Myth ___ Fact

3. The processors and distributors of fish and seafood products must operate under a Seafood HACCP plan.
　___ Myth ✓ Fact

4. Any food that is being purchased is recognized as acceptable for use.
　✓ Myth ___ Fact

5. A packaged food product is safe from contamination as long as the packaging is not torn, ripped, or open.
　✓ Myth ___ Fact

Purchasing Food from Approved Sources

Purchasing food from unsafe suppliers is one of the five most common risk factors to food safety according to the CDC. Food must be purchased from legally approved and reputable suppliers. These suppliers must meet the delivery and transportation standards of the operation. Delivery and transportation standards may include product handling, temperature controls, and schedules. Suppliers of approved food, food ingredients, and food packaging are required to operate their business to meet food safety production requirements and to produce product that meets established labeling identity standards. Supplier regulatory inspections and voluntary food safety audits, as well as in-house quality assurance or control programs, are used to ensure that suppliers are meeting regulatory and quality requirements.

Food Standards

Different agencies inspect and regulate food suppliers based on the type of product produced or handled. Inspection agencies include the:

- USDA – meat and poultry products and egg grading;
- FDA – juice, dairy, seafood, other food products and ingredients;
- Local or state health or agriculture departments; and
- Other federal, state, and local agencies for particular foods or products.

Commercially produced foods will be labeled to meet the requirements specific for the type of food being produced. Federal laws that impact the production of food are published in the Code of Federal Regulations (CFR).

Food labeling can include the following:

- Quality standards
    - Milk and dairy products: Grade A
    - Eggs: Grades AA, A, and B
    - Meat: Prime, choice
    - Olive oil: Virgin, extra virgin
- Consumer handling or cooking instruction
    - Eggs, meat, poultry, and commercially processed frozen foods all require specific consumer preparation and handling instructions to prevent illness.
- Nutritional information
- Allergen information
- Ingredients and all sub ingredients
- Weight and volume
- Source of the food – such as where shellfish are harvested

- Special treatment for pathogen control – foods labeled as cooked, pasteurized, irradiated, frozen for parasite destruction safety

Supplier documentation for foods received must provide clear and accurate information concerning the product. Proper documentation can include invoices, purchase orders, and shellstock identification tags.

Foods of Special Concern

Fish

Fish purchased for sale or service must be commercially and legally caught or harvested. The processors and distributors of fish and seafood products must operate under a Seafood HACCP plan.

If certain raw or undercooked fish is sold by an establishment, the establishment must maintain records from the supplier that the fish has been properly frozen for parasite destruction.

Shellfish

Molluscan shellfish must be purchased from suppliers that meet the requirements of the National Shellfish Sanitation Program to ensure that the shellfish are harvested in safe, clean waters.

- **Molluscan shellfish** are any edible species of fresh or frozen oysters, clams, mussels, and scallops.
- **Shucked shellfish** are molluscan shellfish that have one or both shells removed.

Shellfish harvest area waters can contain microbiological hazards such as Vibrio species pathogens, Hepatitis A virus, and natural toxins. Shellfish require identification tags that record harvest, harvester, and dealer or seller information. Shellstock identification tags must be kept on file for at least 90 days from the sale of the last shellfish.

Wild Mushrooms

Selling or serving wild mushrooms requires expert mushroom identification and can require regulatory approval. Mushrooms must be identified properly in order to avoid consuming mushrooms with toxins. Safety is best met by purchasing wild mushrooms that are grown, harvested, and processed by a regulated provider.

Game Animals

Wild **game animals** can be carriers of many viruses, bacteria, and parasites that may cause illness in humans. Game meat must be purchased from approved suppliers that meet the specifications and requirements of their governing body.

Receiving

Upon delivery of products purchased from approved suppliers, it is critical to inspect the products properly. Inspecting the delivery can include the vehicle, product handling, temperature, condition, and accuracy. Reject any items that were not ordered or do not meet safe standards. The product must look, feel, and smell right. The following chart provides general guidance related to the evaluation of foods when being inspected upon receipt.

Product	Look	Feel	Smell
Meat: Beef, Veal, Pork, Lamb	Bright, not brown, gray, or green	Firm bounce back, no slimy or slippery feel	No off odor
Meat: Pork (bone in)	No black or gray	Firm bounce back, no slimy or slippery feel	No off odor from near bone area
Poultry	Wing tips clear or bright, not darkened or grayed	Firm bounce back, no slimy of slippery feel	No off odor at wing or leg junctures
Fish	No sunken eyes, gills bright not dull	Firm bounce back	No fishy odor
Live Shellfish	Clean, alive	Shell closes when tapped	No off odor
Produce	Clean, no mold, wilting, or discoloring	No slimy or slippery feel	No off odor

Product	Receiving Standards
• Cold foods	• 41°F (5°C) or lower[1]
• Hot foods	• 135°F (57.2°C) or higher[1]
• Live shellfish	• 45°F (7.2°C) or lower[2]
• Shell eggs	• 45°F (7.2°C) or lower[2]
• Frozen foods	• Frozen
• Fresh fish	• Packed with ice
• ROP fish	• 38°F (3.3°C) or ice packed

[1] Internal food temperature
[2] Refrigerated air temperature

Inspecting Products

Products and packaging must be received in good condition. Reject items with evidence of:

- Past use-by or sell-by date;
- Damage, tears, rips, dents or rust on cans, and open seals;
- Soiling;
- Stains or leakage;
- Pests being in the product or contaminating it;
- Having been wet;
- Time/temperature abuse; or
- Mislabeling.

Key Drop Delivery

Key drop delivery occurs when food and products are delivered during non-operating hours, and the supplier or vendor is provided access to the operation so that the product can be brought into the establishment when delivered. When key drop deliveries are permitted, product handling, storage, safety, and security must be carefully evaluated when the establishment returns to operation. It is unsafe and not an acceptable practice if food is left outside the premises.

Recalls

Food may be recalled for different reasons. It will be important to work with the supplier or vendor to know what to do with a recalled food item. Recalled foods must be handled so that they are not sold or served unless the reason for the recall is addressed and the product is safe for use. That is why it is important to have an inventory tracking system. There are three different classes of recalls:

- **Class I:** A food item could cause a serious health problem, maybe even lead to death.
    - Example: *Salmonella enteritidis* is known to be in the eggs.
- **Class II:** A food item could have a less serious or temporary health problem.
    - Example: An allergen is not identified as an ingredient of the product.
- **Class III:** Is unlikely to cause any health problem, but it may not meet a certain standard.
    - Example: A chicken breast is labeled as 6 oz., but it is 4 oz.

Storing

Storage practices followed in a food operation must ensure that food and products are stored in safe and secure locations and is protected from contamination. Common storage practices that ensure that foods are maintained safely include the following:

- Do not store foods in locker rooms, bathrooms, garbage areas, or under unprotected water and sewer lines;
- All storage areas, shelving, and equipment cleaned on a regular basis;
- Food and food related items always kept at least 6 inches (15 cm) off of the floor, away from walls, and protected from contamination;

- All foods labeled with the common name;
- Use-by or sell-by dates clearly included on the label;
- TCS food prepared on site marked with use-by dates not to exceed seven days;
- Frozen foods frozen;
- Cold foods cold: 41°F (5°C) or below;
- Hot foods hot: 135°F (57.2°C) or above;
- Single-use items must be stored in their original packaging;
- Opened and exposed items covered and protected from contamination using food wrap, plastic over-wrap, or lids;
- Dry storage temperatures 50°F - 70°F (10°C - 21.2°C);
- Dry storage relative humidity 50% - 60%; and
- First-in, first-out (FIFO) rotation will ensure that product is used before expiration or use-by date. When new product is received, store it behind products already on the shelves.

Refrigerated Food Storage Practices

Maintaining food product temperature control requires that refrigerators and freezers are working properly. Do not overstock refrigerators or freezers with too much product because it restricts airflow, which can increase food storage temperatures. This could put the food and equipment at risk. When storing raw product in the same cooler, items must be stored properly based on their cooking requirements to minimize cross-contamination. Food items should be stored top to bottom as follows:

1. Ready-to-eat food
2. Fish, steaks, and chops
3. Whole cuts of meat (roasts)
4. Ground meat and ground fish
5. All poultry

Other refrigerated food storage practices or placement requirements include:

- Preventing wet storage of products that are not protected from ice or water contaminants;
- Proper labeling when products are removed from their original packaging;
- Protecting exposed foods during cooling;
- Segregating food to be discarded or returned from food to be used;
- Covering and storing all food items so that dripping and cross-contamination does not occur; and
- Using shelving made of appropriate, cleanable materials, and properly maintaining it.

Chemical Storage

Chemicals must always be stored in a separate area away from food and food-contact surfaces. Chemicals must also be labeled clearly. It is the PIC's responsibility to know who is around the food and chemicals at all times. Monitor and control access to food storage areas to ensure that the food is protected from contamination.

Pop Quiz:
Receiving and Storing
(Check one.)

1. FIFO is a term related to purchasing meats.
___Yes ✓ No

2. Key drop delivery is safe because the food is inspected when delivered.
___Yes ✓ No

3. An invoice with the name of the supplier on it indicates that the supplier is approved.
___Yes ✓ No

4. Foods that are purchased from commercial processors will require different information on the labels based upon the type of food.
✓ Yes ___No

5. Food removed from its original packaging and placed into food containers needs to have these containers labeled with the common name of the food product with a use-by or sell-by date.
✓ Yes ___No

Preparing

Food preparation activities provide numerous opportunities for food to be contaminated or exposed to pathogen growth conditions. When preparing food, be careful to avoid time-temperature abuse and cross-contamination. Cross-contamination from people, hands, gloves, water, equipment, and utensils must be avoided, and proper cleaning procedures must be followed.

Food preparation cross-contamination concerns include:

People

- Restrict access of non-essential personnel in food preparation areas.

Hands

- When preparing food, hands must be clean. Proper handwashing procedures and glove use are needed and must be strictly followed.

Water

- Safe potable water, protected from contamination, must be used and maintained when preparing food and when cleaning hands and food-contact surfaces.

Equipment and Utensils

- Food can only come in contact with clean and sanitized equipment, containers, and utensils, or single-use items. Store utensils in use with the handles above the top of the food and containers.

Temperature Control

- Time/temperature abuse can be minimized by only taking out from temperature control the amount of food that can be used at that time. Pulling out large quantities and preparing large batches of food that will not be used quickly puts the food in the TDZ longer than necessary. Put TCS foods under temperature control as quickly as possible when preparing.
- **Slacking** refers to raising the temperature of the frozen food to enable product dispensing or preparation. Ensure that slacked foods do not exceed 41ºF (5ºC).

Thawing

- To safely thaw frozen food, four methods can be used:

- Refrigerator
  - Place the frozen food in a container and put into the refrigerator.

- Cold running water
  - The water cannot go above 70ºF (21.1ºC), and the frozen food must be submerged under running water.

- Microwave
  - Defrost food in a microwave only if it is going to be cooked immediately.

- Cooking
  - Start cooking the food while it is still frozen.

ROP Fish

Reduced oxygen packaged fish must be opened prior to thawing or at any point during the thawing process. Thawed fish cannot be stored in its unopened ROP packaging.

Fruits and Vegetables

- Raw fruits and vegetables must be thoroughly washed in water (or an approved chemical) to remove soil, pathogens, and chemicals. Pre-cut, bagged produce is often pre-washed and would be indicated on the label. These items are ready-to-eat and do not need further washing.

Juice

- Fresh fruit and vegetable juices packaged for retail sale must be processed according to a HACCP plan. If there is no HACCP plan, the juice package must be labeled with a consumer advisory label warning the customer of the risks. Juices labeled with this warning cannot be served to highly susceptible populations; "WARNING: This product has not been pasteurized and, therefore, may contain harmful bacteria that can cause serious illness in children, the elderly, and persons with weakened immune systems."

Labeling and Date Marking

- Foods prepared on-site for retail sale must be labeled with all ingredient information (in weight order), nutritional information, use-by or sell-by dates, and all other information required to identify the food being sold.

- Any food removed from its original packaging must be labeled with proper identifying information.

- TCS food that is prepared on-site to be held longer than 24 hours, or opened commercially prepared food, must be marked with a discard date not to exceed seven days. If this food product is not sold or consumed within the discard date time period, then it must be properly discarded.
    - When combining ingredients, the use-by or sell-by date does not reset. The food item is only as fresh as the oldest ingredient in the product.
- There are numerous labels and labeling techniques that food service and retail establishments use for date marking.
    - Operations may use color coding, preprinted labels, UPC codes, or other methods.

Pop Quiz:
Food Labeling
(Check one.)

1. Food products for retail sale must be labeled with the ingredients.
   ✓ Yes ___ No

2. Food ingredients on a label must be in alphabetical order.   weight
   ___ Yes ✓ No

3. Sell-by or use-by dates are required for all foods.
   ✓ Yes ___ No

4. In-house prepared TCS foods can have any sell-by or use-by date.
   ___ Yes ✓ No

5. Packaged fresh-squeezed juice only requires a warning label when being sold to a facility that will serve immune-compromised populations.
   ___ Yes ✓ No

Chapter 7
Food Code Definitions

- **Fish:** fresh or saltwater finfish, crustaceans and other forms of aquatic life (including alligator, frog, aquatic turtle, jellyfish, sea cucumber, and sea urchin and the roe of such animals) other than birds or mammals, and all mollusks, if such animal life is intended for human consumption.

- **Food:** a raw, cooked, or processed edible substance, ice, beverage, or ingredient used or intended for use or for sale in whole or in part for human consumption, or chewing gum.

- **Game animal:** an animal, the products of which are food, that is not classified as livestock, sheep, swine, goat, horse, mule, or other equine in 9 CFR 301.2 Definitions, or as poultry or fish. Game animals include mammals such as reindeer, elk, deer, antelope, water buffalo, bison, rabbit, squirrel, opossum, raccoon, nutria, or muskrat, and non-aquatic reptiles such as land snakes. Game animal does not include ratites.

- **Grade A standards:** the requirements of the United States Public Health Service/FDA "Grade A Pasteurized Milk Ordinance" with which certain fluid and dry milk and milk products comply.

- **Juice:** the aqueous liquid expressed or extracted from one or more fruits or vegetables, purées of the edible portions of one or more fruits or vegetables, or any concentrates of such liquid or purée. Juice does not include, for purposes of HACCP, liquids, purées, or concentrates that are not used as beverages or ingredients of beverages.

- **Meat:** the flesh of animals used as food including the dressed flesh of cattle, swine, sheep, or goats and other edible animals, except fish, poultry, and wild game animals as specified under subparagraphs 3-201.17(A) (3) and (4).

- **Molluscan shellfish:** any edible species of fresh or frozen oysters, clams, mussels, and scallops or edible portions thereof, except when the scallop product consists only of the shucked adductor muscle.

- **Packaged:** bottled, canned, cartoned, bagged, or wrapped, whether packaged in a food establishment or a food processing plant. Packaged does not include a wrapper, carry-out box, or other nondurable container used to containerize food for the purpose of facilitating food protection during service and receipt of the food by the consumer.

- **Shellstock:** raw, in-shell molluscan shellfish.

- **Shucked shellfish:** molluscan shellfish that have one or both shells removed.

- **Slacking:** the process of moderating the temperature of a food, such as allowing a food to gradually increase from a temperature of -10°F (-23°C) to 25°F (-4°C) in preparation for deep-fat frying or to facilitate even heat penetration during the cooking of previously block-frozen food such as shrimp.

- **USDA:** the U.S. Department of Agriculture.

Chapter 7
Conclusion

To accomplish the sale and service of safe food, the PIC must make food safety a priority, from the initial purchase through subsequent handling to final preparation of the food for consumption. This concept is often expressed using the phrase "farm to fork." Preparing safe food is a process that not only focuses on actual food preparation practices but also must include every handling step involved including receiving and storing of food.

Chapter 7

Check for Understanding
(Circle one.)

1. When preparing a TCS food on-site, the prepared food item can be held up to _____.

    a. 3 days

    b. 5 days

    c. 7 days

    d. 9 days

2. Nutritional labeling requirements can apply to food made on-site when the food is _____.

    a. being prepared daily for customer self-service

    b. being prepared for individual service

    c. sold as a take-out food item

    d. packaged and sold on retail display shelves

3. When thawing foods using running water, the temperature cannot exceed _____.

    a. 70°F (21.1°C)

    b. 80°F (26.6°C)

    c. 90°F (32.2°C)

    d. 100°F (37.7°C)

4. When storing raw food in a refrigerator, ground beef must be stored above _____.

    a. lettuce

    b. poultry

    c. fish

    d. pork chops

5. Food recalls can happen with any food product for a variety of reasons. A Class I recall means that the food item _____.

    a. can cause an allergic reaction for an ingredient not listed on the label

    b. can cause serious illness

    c. can present a temporary health problem

    d. has an incorrect label weight

6. Live shellfish can be received at a maximum refrigerated air temperature of _____.
   a. 32°F (0°C)
   b. 41°F (5°C)
   c. 45°F (7.2°C)
   d. 70°F (21.1°C)

7. Which of the following will cause concern when observed during receiving?
   a. Purchase order, invoice, and proper count on inspection are a match
   b. Frozen products have discoloring on the left side corners of the product packaging
   c. The product use-by date is printed on the bottom of the product label instead of on the top
   d. The delivery vehicle driver identifies himself, shows identification, and presents delivery paperwork

8. Approved food suppliers are identified by their ability to demonstrate that they operate _____.
   a. with great customer service representatives
   b. without Better Business Bureau complaints
   c. in compliance with the regulatory authority
   d. with product testing certifications

9. Commercially processed foods will be labeled with nutritional information, weight and volume, and _____.
   a. allergen information
   b. recipe information
   c. biological hazards
   d. chemical hazards

10. Fresh pork bone-in roasts are properly checked at receiving for freshness by _____.
   a. taking the temperature to ensure that it does not exceed 48°F (8.9°C)
   b. verifying that the color of the meat is not black or gray
   c. observing whether the meat is slippery or slimy
   d. touching the roast and it does not bounce back

FDA Food Code References

Chapter 3 – Food
- 3-1 Characteristics
    - 3-101 Condition
    - 3-101.11 Safe, Unadulterated, and Honestly Presented
- 3-2 Sources, Specifications, and Original Containers and Records
    - 3-201.11 Compliance with Food Law
    - 3-201.12 Food in a Hermetically Sealed Container
    - 3-201.13 Fluid Milk and Milk Products
    - 3-201.14 Fish
    - 3-201.15 Molluscan Shellfish
    - 3-201.16 Wild Mushrooms
    - 3-201.17 Game Animals
    - 3-202 Specifications for Receiving
    - 3-202.11 Temperature
    - 3-202.12 Additives
    - 3-202.13 Eggs
    - 3-202.14 Eggs and Milk Products, Pasteurized
    - 3-202.15 Package Integrity
    - 3-202.16 Ice

- 3-202.17 Shucked Shellfish, Packaging and Identification
- 3-202.18 Shellstock Identification
- 3-202.19 Shellstock, Condition
- 3-202.110 Juice Treated
- 3-203 Original Containers and Records
- 3-203.11 Molluscan Shellfish, Original Container
- 3-203.12 Shellstock, Maintaining Identification

• 3-3 Protection from Contamination After Receiving
- 3-301 Preventing Contamination by Employees
- 3-301.12 Preventing Contamination When Tasting
- 3-302 Preventing Food and Ingredient Contamination
- 3-302.11 Packaged and Unpackaged Food – Separation, Packaging, and Segregation
- 3-302.12 Food Storage Containers, Identified with Common Name of Food
- 3-302.13 Pasteurized Eggs, Substitute for Raw Eggs for Certain Recipes
- 3-302.14 Protection from Unapproved Additives
- 3-302.15 Washing Fruits and Vegetables
- 3-303 Preventing Contamination from Ice Used as a Coolant
- 3-303.11 Ice Used as Exterior Coolant, Prohibited as Ingredient
- 3-303.12 Storage or Display of Food in Contact with Water or Ice
- 3-304 Preventing Contamination from Equipment, Utensils, and Linens
- 3-304.11 Food Contact with Equipment and Utensils
- 3-304.12 In-Use Utensils, Between-Use Storage
- 3-304.13 Linens and Napkins, Use Limitation
- 3-304.14 Wiping Cloths, Use Limitation
- 3-305 Preventing Contamination from the Premises
- 3-305.11 Food Storage
- 3-305.12 Food Storage, Prohibited Areas
- 3-305.13 Vended Time/Temperature Control for Safety Food, Original Container
- 3-305.14 Food Preparation
- 3-307 Preventing Contamination from Other Sources
- 3-307.11 Miscellaneous Sources of Contamination

• 3-5 Limitation of Growth of Organisms of Public Health Concern
- 3-501 Temperature and Time Control
- 3-501.11 Frozen Food
- 3-501.12 Time/Temperature Control for Safety Food, Slacking
- 3-501.13 Thawing
- 3-501.16 Time/Temperature Control for Safety Food, Hot and Cold Holding

• 3-6 Food Identity, Presentation, and On-premises Labeling
- 3-601 Accurate Representation
- 3-601.11 Standards of Identity
- 3-601.12 Honestly Presented

Chapter 8:
Proper Cooking for Food Service and Retail Establishments

Chapter 8: Goals

In this chapter, participants will learn to:

- Define the different categories of foods that will require different internal cooking temperatures and time combinations to ensure safety.
- Identify different types of cooking methods that require unique cooking procedures.
- Apply correct minimum internal cooking temperatures to ensure the sale or service of safe foods.
- Understand the three methods for freezing fish to kill naturally occurring harmful parasites.
- Recognize the importance of consumer advisories, children's menus, and properly cooking food for highly susceptible populations.

Chapter 8: Myth or Fact

(Check one.)

1. All foods that are normally cooked in order to reduce pathogens to safe levels are safe to eat when not fully cooked as long as the customer is informed.
   ✓ Myth ___ Fact

2. The Food Code requires that all meat products be cooked using the same cooking temperature and time.
   ✓ Myth ___ Fact

3. An effective way to make food that contains harmful parasites safe is to freeze the food.
   ___ Myth ✓ Fact

4. A TCS food must reach a minimum internal cooking temperature for a minimum amount of time in order to ensure that the food is safe to consume.
   ___ Myth ✓ Fact

5. Foods on a children's menu should not include raw or undercooked TCS foods.
   ___ Myth ✓ Fact

Cooking

Failing to cook food adequately is one of the five most common risk factors to food safety according to the CDC. Cooking TCS foods to minimum internal cooking temperatures and time is done to reduce pathogens to safe levels. Minimum cooking time/temperature combinations for TCS foods only guarantee safety when:

- Foods are properly handled to limit microorganism growth prior to being cooked; and
- Foods are not contaminated with unexpected additional types or numbers of pathogens.

Minimum Internal Cooking Temperatures and Times

- **135°F (57.2°C)**
    - Heat-treated plant foods for hot holding
    - Commercially processed foods for hot holding

- **145°F (62.8°C) for 4 minutes**
    - Meat – whole-muscle* cuts (roasts)

- **145°F (62.8°C) for 15 seconds**
    - Meat – steaks or chops
    - Fish*/shellfish
    - Eggs – for immediate service
    - Commercially raised game meat

- **155°F (68.3°C) for 15 seconds**
    - Ground (comminuted*) meat (and mechanically tenderized* or injected meats)
    - Ground (comminuted) fish
    - Eggs – hot held
    - Ratites* (emu, ostrich, and rhea)
    - Ground (comminuted) game meat

- **165°F (73.9°C) for 15 seconds**
    - Poultry* – whole and ground
    - Stuffing and stuffed foods
    - TCS animal foods cooked in a microwave
    - Wild game animals* that are live caught
    - Previously cooked TCS ingredients
    - Baluts*

*See Chapter 8 Food Code Definitions.

Food characteristics, such as size, fat and moisture content, and humidity during cooking affect cooking temperature requirements for ensuring food safety. For meat roasts, these characteristics require using different cooking parameters based upon the meat roast size, cooking method, and time/temperature combination used. The following charts provide these different cooking parameters for meat roasts.

Cooking Method and Meat Roast Size Chart

Oven Type	Oven Temperature Based on Roast Weight	
	Less than 10 lbs. (4.5 kg)	10 lbs. (4.5 kg) or more
Still Dry	350°F (177°C) or more	250°F (121°C) or more
Convection	325°F (163°C) or more	250°F (121°C) or more
High Humidity[1]	250°F (121°C) or less	250°F (121°C) or less

[1] Relative humidity greater than 90% for at least one hour as measured in the cooking chamber or exit of the oven; or in a moisture-impermeable bag that provides 100% humidity.

Different safe cooking time/temperature combinations for meat roasts are represented in the following chart. For example, the chart indicates that cooking a beef roast for 112 minutes after it has reached 130°F (54.4°C) provides the same safety level when cooked for four minutes after it has reached 145°F (62.8°C).

Equivalent Cooking Time/Temperature Combinations Chart

Temperature		Time[1] in Minutes	Temperature		Time[1] in Seconds
°F	(°C)		°F	(°C)	
130°F	(54.4°C)	112	147°F	(63.9°C)	134
131°F	(55.0°C)	89	149°F	(65.0°C)	85
133°F	(56.1°C)	56	151°F	(66.1°C)	54
135°F	(57.2°C)	36	153°F	(67.2°C)	34
136°F	(57.8°C)	28	155°F	(68.3°C)	22
138°F	(58.9°C)	18	157°F	(69.4°C)	14
140°F	(60.0°C)	12	158°F	(70.0°C)	0
142°F	(61.1°C)	8			
144°F	(62.2°C)	5			
145°F	(62.8°C)	4			

[1] Holding time may include post-oven heat rise.

Special Cooking Considerations

Microwave Cooking of Raw Animal Foods (Fish, Eggs, Meat, and Poultry)

1. Cover foods to retain moisture.
2. Rotate foods at least once midway through the cooking process.
3. Let the food sit covered for two minutes before checking the temperature.
4. Cook to internal temperature of 165°F (73.9°C) for 15 seconds.

Non-Continuous Cooking

Non-continuous cooking (partial cooking) of animal foods prior to final cooking must be done safely. Pathogens can survive partial cooking and multiply during cooling, holding, and future preparation before final cooking. To prevent unsafe conditions when using a non-continuous cooking method, food must be:

- Heated initially for no longer than 60 minutes.
- Cooled after initial heating to less than 70°F (21.1°C) within two hours, and cooled to less than 41°F (5.0°C) within the next four hours.
- Held frozen or cold at 41°F (5.0°C) or lower.
- Cooked to the required minimum internal temperature and time prior to sale or service.

Using this method of cooking may require prior approval by the regulatory authority and a written plan. The written plan must provide details for each step in the handling process. Specific time and temperature parameters used to control biological hazards from pathogen survival and growth must be included.

Monitoring Cooking Temperatures

It is essential to check final cooking temperatures to ensure that safe temperatures are reached. When checking temperatures, it is important to:

1. Use a calibrated, cleaned, and sanitized thermometer.
2. Check the temperature in the thickest part of the food.
3. Check the temperature in two parts of the food to make sure that there is an even cooking temperature throughout the item.

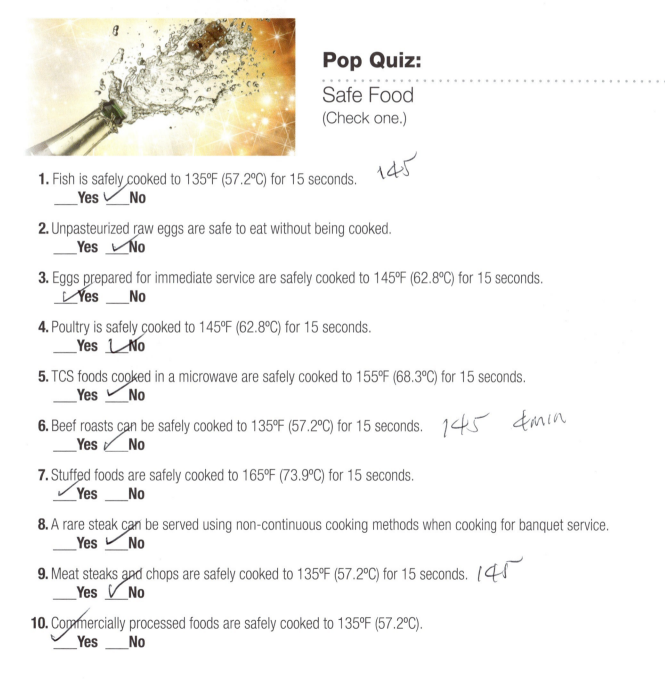

Pop Quiz:
Safe Food
(Check one.)

1. Fish is safely cooked to 135°F (57.2°C) for 15 seconds. *145*
   ___ Yes ✓ No

2. Unpasteurized raw eggs are safe to eat without being cooked.
   ___ Yes ✓ No

3. Eggs prepared for immediate service are safely cooked to 145°F (62.8°C) for 15 seconds.
   ✓ Yes ___ No

4. Poultry is safely cooked to 145°F (62.8°C) for 15 seconds.
   ___ Yes ✓ No

5. TCS foods cooked in a microwave are safely cooked to 155°F (68.3°C) for 15 seconds.
   ___ Yes ✓ No

6. Beef roasts can be safely cooked to 135°F (57.2°C) for 15 seconds. *145 4min*
   ___ Yes ✓ No

7. Stuffed foods are safely cooked to 165°F (73.9°C) for 15 seconds.
   ✓ Yes ___ No

8. A rare steak can be served using non-continuous cooking methods when cooking for banquet service.
   ___ Yes ✓ No

9. Meat steaks and chops are safely cooked to 135°F (57.2°C) for 15 seconds. *145*
   ___ Yes ✓ No

10. Commercially processed foods are safely cooked to 135°F (57.2°C).
    ✓ Yes ___ No

Non-Cooking Destruction of Pathogens

Freezing fish kills naturally occurring harmful parasites. This allows for uncooked fish that is raw, raw marinated, partially cooked, or marinated and partially cooked, to be safe when eaten. Freezing fish using one of the following three methods will provide the same safety as proper cooking.

Method 1: Freeze and store at a temperature of -4°F (-20°C) or below for a minimum of 168 hours (seven days).

Method 2: Freeze and store at a temperature of -31°F (-35°C) or below for a minimum of 15 hours.

Method 3: Freeze until frozen fish reaches the temperature of -31°F (-35°C) or below and then maintain storage temperature of -4°F (-20°C) or below for a minimum of 24 hours.

Documentation and records for fish that will be consumed raw must be maintained for at least **90 days** after sale or service. The information retained must identify that the fish was frozen using **one of the three approved methods** or provide information that identifies the safety of the fish without treatment.

Fish

Specific fish that do not require the freezing treatment before uncooked consumption include:

1. Molluscan shellfish;

2. Tuna species
   - *Thunnus alalunga* (albacore)
   - *Thunnus albacares* (yellowfin tuna)
   - *Thunnus atlanticus* (blackfin)
   - *Thunnus maccoyii* (bluefin tuna, southern)
   - *Thunnus obesus* (bigeye tuna)
   - *Thunnus thynnus* (bluefin tuna, northern)

3. Aquacultured fish such as salmon, that:
   a. If raised in open water, are raised in net pens, or
   b. Are raised in land-based operations such as ponds or tanks, and
   c. Are fed formulated feed, such as pellets, that contains no live parasites infective to the aquacultured fish.

4. Fish eggs that have been removed from the skin and rinsed.

Consumer Advisories

Cooking foods to their required minimum internal cooking temperature will destroy the pathogens. Foods that are cooked below their required cooking temperature can be served, as long as a consumer advisory is provided. A consumer advisory includes a **disclosure** to identify the food and a **reminder** which informs the customer of the foodborne illness risk associated with consuming raw or undercooked foods. The advisory should be posted on a menu, place card, or other effective written means.

Children's Menu

Preschool-aged children are highly susceptible to a foodborne illness. To prevent illness children's menu foods should not include raw or undercooked TCS foods.

Highly Susceptible Populations

Food operations that serve primarily **highly susceptible populations**, such as nursing homes or hospitals, cannot use a consumer advisory nor serve any raw or undercooked animal foods. Foods at these locations must be cooked to the required minimum internal cooking temperature.

Pop Quiz:
Safe Food Overview
(Check one.)

1. Foods that are cooked below their required cooking temperature can be served without a consumer advisory.
   ___ Yes ✓ No

2. Freezing fish, to kill naturally occurring harmful parasites, permits uncooked fish that is raw, raw and marinated, partially cooked, or marinated and partially cooked, to be safe when eaten.
   ✓ Yes ___ No

3. Children's menu foods should include raw or undercooked TCS foods.
   ___ Yes ✓ No

4. One method of freezing fish involves freezing and storing at a temperature of -4°F (-20°C) or below for a minimum of 15 hours.
   ___ Yes ✓ No

5. Documentation and records for fish that will be consumed raw must be maintained for at least 60 days after sale or service.
   ___ Yes ✓ No

Chapter 8
Food Code Definitions

- **Balut:** an embryo inside a fertile egg that has been incubated for a period sufficient for the embryo to reach a specific stage of development, after which it is removed from incubation before hatching.

- **Comminuted:** reduced in size by methods including chopping, flaking, grinding, or mincing. Comminuted includes fish or meat products that are reduced in size and restructured or reformulated such as gefilte fish, gyros, ground beef, and sausage; and a mixture of two or more types of meat that has been reduced in size and combined, such as sausages made from two or more meats.

- **Disclosure:** a written statement that clearly identifies the animal-derived foods which are, or can be ordered, raw, undercooked, or without otherwise being processed to eliminate pathogens, or items that contain an ingredient that is raw, undercooked, or without otherwise being processed to eliminate pathogens.

- **Fish:** fresh or saltwater finfish, crustaceans and other forms of aquatic life (including alligator, frog, aquatic turtle, jellyfish, sea cucumber, and sea urchin and the roe of such animals) other than birds or mammals, and all mollusks, if such animal life is intended for human consumption. Fish includes an edible human food product derived in whole or in part from fish, including fish that have been processed in any manner.

- **Game animal:** an animal, the products of which are food, that is not classified as livestock, sheep, swine, goat, horse, mule, or other equine in 9 CFR 301.2 Definitions, or as poultry, or fish. Game animals include mammals such as reindeer, elk, deer, antelope, water buffalo, bison, rabbit, squirrel, opossum, raccoon, nutria, or muskrat, and nonaquatic reptiles such as land snakes. Game animals do not include ratites.

- **Mechanically tenderized:** manipulating meat with deep penetration by processes that may be referred to as "blade tenderizing," "jaccarding," "pinning," "needling," or using blades, pins, needles or any mechanical device. Mechanically tenderized does not include processes by which solutions are injected into meat.

- **Non-continuous cooking:** the cooking of food in a food establishment using a process in which the initial heating of the food is intentionally halted so that it may be cooled and held for complete cooking at a later time prior to sale or service. Non-continuous cooking does not include cooking procedures that only involve temporarily interrupting or slowing an otherwise continuous cooking process.

- **Poultry:** any domesticated bird (chickens, turkeys, ducks, geese, guineas, ratites, or squabs), whether live or dead, as defined in 9 CFR 381.1 Poultry Products Inspection Regulations Definitions, Poultry; and any migratory waterfowl or game bird, pheasant, partridge, quail, grouse, or pigeon, whether live or dead, as defined in 9 CFR 362.1 Voluntary Poultry Inspection Regulations Definitions.

- **Ratite:** a flightless bird such as an emu, ostrich, or rhea.

- **Reminder:** a written statement concerning the health risk of consuming animal foods raw, undercooked, or without otherwise being processed to eliminate pathogens.

- **Whole-muscle, intact beef:** whole-muscle beef that is not injected, mechanically tenderized, reconstructed, or scored and marinated, from which beef steaks may be cut.

Chapter 8
Conclusion

The PIC is responsible for ensuring that raw foods are properly cooked or frozen at specific times and temperatures to reduce pathogens to safe levels. Raw foods that are not treated to reduce pathogens must not be served to individuals that are at high risk for becoming sick from pathogens. Individuals who are deemed healthy need to be made aware of the risk of getting ill from foods being served and sold that are likely to contain pathogens because they were not properly cooked or frozen.

Chapter 8

Check for Understanding
(Circle one.)

1. A minimum safe cooking temperature of 155°F (68.3°C) for 15 seconds is appropriate for _____.
    a. turkey burgers
    b. lasagna
    c. pork chops
    d. hamburgers

2. The minimum safe cooking temperature for eggs for hot holding is _____.
    a. 135°F (57.2°C) for 15 seconds
    b. 145°F (62.8°C) for 15 seconds
    c. 155°F (68.3°C) for 15 seconds
    d. 165°F (73.9°C) for 15 seconds

3. A minimum safe cooking temperature of 165°F (73.9°C) for 15 seconds is appropriate for _____.
    a. fried eggs for a customer order
    b. stuffed pork chops
    c. steamed crabs
    d. commercially raised ground game meat

4. A minimum safe cooking temperature of 165°F (73.9°C) for 15 seconds is not required for _____.
    a. microwave-cooked foods
    b. hot turkey sausage
    c. ostrich meat
    d. meat-stuffed pasta

5. The minimum safe cooking temperature for fish is _____.
    a. 135°F (57.2°C) for 15 seconds
    b. 145°F (62.8°C) for 15 seconds
    c. 155°F (68.3°C) for 15 seconds
    d. 165°F (73.9°C) for 15 seconds

6. Food operations in a nursing home that prepare and serve eggs for immediate service are permitted to do so when _____.
    a. eggs are cooked to 145°F (62.8°C) for 15 seconds
    b. a consumer advisory is posted in plain sight in the dining room
    c. eggs are cooked to 135°F (57.2°C) for 15 seconds
    d. eggs are cooked to 140°F (60°C) for 15 seconds

7. Poultry requires a minimum cooking temperature of _____.

    a. 135°F (57.2°C) for 15 seconds

    b. 145°F (62.8°C) for 15 seconds

    c. 155°F (68.3°C) for 15 seconds

    d. 165°F (73.9°C) for 15 seconds

8. When cooking animal foods using a microwave, which step is inaccurate?

    a. Cook to internal temperature of 165°F (73.9°C) for 15 seconds.

    b. Rotate foods at least once midway through the cooking process.

    c. Cover foods to retain moisture.

    d. Serve within 30 seconds to ensure that the food items stay hot for service.

9. TCS animal foods cooked in a microwave require a minimum internal cooking temperature of _____.

    a. 135°F (57.2°C) for 15 seconds

    b. 145°F (62.8°C) for 15 seconds

    c. 155°F (68.3°C) for 15 seconds

    d. 165°F (73.9°C) for 15 seconds

10. _____ fish to kill harmful parasites can be done safely using an approved method.

    a. Washing

    b. Freezing

    c. Cooling

    d. all of the above

FDA Food Code References

Chapter 3 – Food

- 3-4 Destruction of Organisms of Public Health Concern Cooking
- 3-401 Cooking
    - 3-401.11 Raw Animal Foods
    - 3-401.12 Microwave Cooking
    - 3-401.13 Plant Food Cooking for Hot Holding
    - 3-401.14 Non-Continuous Cooking of Raw Animal Foods
- 3-402 Freezing
    - 3-402.11 Parasite Destruction
    - 3-402.12 Records, Creation and Retention

Chapter 9:
Proper Holding for Food Service and Retail Establishments

Chapter 9: Goals

In this chapter, participants will learn to:

- Apply temperature requirements to the safe holding of food.
- Define time as a public health control.
- Identify safe food cooling methods.
- Understand proper reheating requirements.
- Recognize improper and proper practices for serving food on-site, off-site, and in self-service areas.

Chapter 9: Myth or Fact

(Check one.)

1. Cold food can be held without temperature control for up to six hours, as long as the food does not go above 70ºF (21.1ºC). If the food reaches 70ºF (21.1ºC), it must be discarded.
   ___Myth ✓Fact

2. When reheating cold food for hot holding, the reheating process can take up to four hours.
   ✓Myth ___Fact

3. Commercial refrigeration equipment is designed to hold cold food temperatures and cool large masses of food.
   ✓Myth ___Fact

4. While cold holding or hot holding food, it is not necessary to keep foods covered.
   ✓Myth ___Fact

5. When food is being held prior to sale or service, it is important to check the temperature of held foods at least every four hours.
   ___Myth ✓Fact

Hot and Cold Holding

Holding food at incorrect temperatures is one of the five most common risk factors to food safety according to the CDC. Foods being held for sale or service must be held at temperatures out of the temperature danger zone to prevent pathogen growth or toxin production.

- Cold foods must be held at 41°F (5°C) or below; and
- Hot foods must be held at 135°F (57.2°C) or above.

When food is being held prior to sale or service, it is important to check the temperature at least every four hours. This is done to ensure that the food temperature has not risen or fallen to a temperature that will support pathogen growth. If the temperatures are checked every four hours and the food is found to be in the TDZ, then the food must be discarded. However, checking food temperatures every two hours is recommended in order to provide an opportunity for a corrective action. If the food is found to be between 41°F and 135°F (5°C and 57.2°C), then cool or reheat the food to maintain safe holding temperatures.

While holding food, keep it covered or protected in order to reduce the chance of any contamination, and to help maintain the temperature of the food.

Time as a Public Health Control

Food operations that follow a written plan to hold food without using equipment to maintain temperatures can use time to keep food safe. When using **time as a public health control**, written procedures with the necessary details are required. These details explain how food is prepared and handled to meet safety requirements. This procedure will require that food be labeled with the time that the food was removed from temperature control and the time that the food must be discarded. There are two options when using time as a public health control:

- **4 Hour Holding** - Hot or cold food can be held without temperature control for up to 4 hours if:
    - The food is labeled with discard time; and
    - The food is served or discarded within 4 hours.

- **6 Hour Holding** - Cold food can be held without temperature control for up to 6 hours if:
    - The food is labeled with discard time;
    - The food is discarded if it goes above 70°F (21.1°C); and
    - The food is served or discarded within 6 hours.

Time as a Public Health Control

Food service and retail establishments can use visual props to indicate the time for holding foods when permitted. These props can be substituted for labels on food that have the exact time frame. They must be visible to the food employee when using or dispensing food without temperature control.

Cooling

Cooling is done when foods that are hot or warm need to be cooled for holding and future use. It is important to cool foods properly so that pathogens do not have the opportunity to produce toxins or grow and reach unsafe levels.

Commercial refrigeration equipment is designed to hold cold food. It is not designed to cool large quantities of food. Putting hot foods in refrigerators or freezers puts the food and the equipment at risk. Rapid chilling can be done in equipment designed to cool food to acceptable temperatures quickly. Tumble chillers cool by using very low-temperature water, and blast chillers use low-temperature air and high rates of air circulation.

Use one or more of the proper cooling methods and procedures to help remove heat:

- Cut foods into smaller pieces;
- Place foods into shallow pans;
- Use ice as an ingredient;
- Place food into a container and into an ice water bath;
- Stir food;
- Use an ice paddle; or
- Use rapid cool equipment, such as a blast chiller.

Food containers used when cooling foods in equipment need to be:

1. Arranged with proper spacing and airflow;
2. In shallow, stainless steel containers;
3. In single layers and not stacked; and
4. Loosely covered (or uncovered if protected from overhead contamination).

These things are done to speed up the cooling process.

Two-Stage Cooling Time Requirements

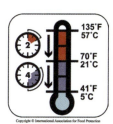

Cooling TCS foods safely requires a two-stage approach with a maximum time of six hours to cool food from 135°F to 41°F (57.2°C to 5°C) or lower. The first stage for cooling cooked foods is the most critical step of the hot food cooling process.

- **Stage 1:** 135°F to 70°F (57.2°C to 21.1°C) within two hours.
- **Stage 2:** 70°F to 41°F (21.1°C to 5°C) or lower within four hours.

Food prepared at ambient (room) temperature, such as tuna salad prepared with canned tuna, must be cooled to 41°F (5°C) within four hours.

When cooling food, it is important to monitor the temperature to be sure that the time requirements are met. Cooling foods from 135°F to 41°F (57.2°C to 5°C) can take a total of six hours. But, if using the two-stage cooling method and the food does not reach 70°F (21.1°C) within two hours, or 41°F (5°C) within six hours, then a corrective action is needed. The corrective action can be to discard or reheat the food to 165°F (73.9°C) for 15 seconds within two hours. Once reheated properly, then recool within the proper time and temperature criteria.

Developing Cooling Procedures

When developing a specific cooling process, it is critical to test, monitor, and keep records to prove that the cooling process works. This will determine the proper equipment, timing, and procedures needed for the process.

Reheating

When reheating previously cooked TCS foods for hot holding, the following temperatures must be reached:

- 165°F (73.9°C) for 15 seconds within two hours for food that is cooked, cooled, and reheated.
    - Food must stand for two minutes after reheating in a microwave.
- 135°F (57.2°C) within two hours for ready-to-eat food that is commercially processed.

Foods that will be consumed immediately and not held do not have any temperature requirements, assuming that the food was initially cooked, cooled, and stored properly.

Pop Quiz:

Temperatures
(Complete.)

Match the process with the correct temperature required. Place the correct letter in the space provided.

Process

1. __d__ Cold Holding Food
2. __c__ Hot Food Time as a Public Health Control
3. __a__ Cooling Food
4. __e__ Cold Food Time as a Public Health Control
5. __b__ Hot Holding Food

Temperature Requirement

a. 135°F to 70°F (57.2°C to 21.1°C) within two hours; then 70°F to 41°F (21.1°C to 5°C) or lower within four hours

b. 135°F (57.2°C) or above

c. 135°F (57.2°C) or above (then removed from heat) for up to four hours

d. 41°F (5°C) or below

e. 41°F (5°C) or below, (then removed from cold) for up to six hours, as long as the food does not go above 70°F (21.1°C)

Serving

When serving food, it is important to follow good personal hygiene procedures and use serving equipment properly.

Always:

- Hold tableware by the handles.
    - Never touch the food contact area.
- Carry plates without stacking, and only touch the edge or bottom.
    - Never touch the top of a plate.
- Hold the bottom, stem, or handle of cups and glasses.
    - Never touch the rim.

- Use an ice scoop when scooping ice.
    - Never use hands or the drinking container.
- Use gloves, tongs, or deli tissue when handling ready-to-eat food.
    - Never touch with bare hands.
- Use only one clean serving utensil for one food item at a time.
    - This will prevent cross-contamination of pathogens, allergens, and flavors.
- Clean and sanitize utensils and equipment at least every four hours if they are in constant use.
    - This will prevent any pathogens from remaining on the utensil in the temperature danger zone for more than four hours.

- Use clean linens and napkins when lining a container for the service of foods.
    - Never reuse linens or napkins.
- Use clean bus trays and carts.
    - Never serve off of contaminated surfaces.

Re-service

Re-service is the transfer of food that is unused and returned by a customer, after being served or sold and in the possession of the consumer, to another person. There is only one item that is allowed to be re-served to customers, which is packaged food. This means that if an unused food item given to one customer is in a sealed package (such as crackers, mustard, or salad dressing), it can be given to another customer.

Never re-serve or reuse:

- Leftover rolls;
- Returned foods that were prepared improperly (such as grilled fish instead of baked fish); or
- Garnishes, such as parsley, pickles, or lemons.

Pop Quiz:

Service
(Check one.)

1. Use tongs to pick up and serve rolls.
   ✓ Yes ___ No

2. Grasp glasses at the stem or bottom.
   ✓ Yes ___ No

3. Carry plates with only touching the top.
   ___ Yes ✓ No

4. Use hands to gently scoop ice into a glass.
   ___ Yes ✓ No

5. Hold eating utensils by the handles.
   ✓ Yes ___ No

Self-Service Areas

There may be times when customers can serve themselves, such as at a buffet or salad bar. Customers are not trained in proper food handling, so it is very important to monitor these areas and discard any food that may have become contaminated. To prevent customer contamination of food, requirements at self-service areas include:

- Labeling all foods for easy identification;
- Having a designated serving utensil for each item to avoid cross-contamination;
- Preventing customers from refilling used plates, bowls, cups, etc.;
- Using approved refillable containers only when a contamination-free process is in use;
- Using dispensers and holders to protect utensils, bowls, plates, cups, etc. from contamination;
- Keeping condiments in dispensers designed to protect them, and keeping foods being provided in original containers, individual portions, packets, or containers that protect the food;
- Requiring that sneeze guards extend 7 inches (17.7 cm) away from food and 14 inches (35.6 cm) above the food; and
- Protecting food on display by the use of packaging, counters, service lines, sneeze guards, display cases, or other effective means. Some exceptions include nuts in the shell and whole, raw fruits and vegetables that are intended for hulling, peeling, or washing by the customer before consumption.

Raw, unpackaged animal food, such as beef, lamb, pork, poultry, and fish, unless a ready-to-eat food such as sushi or raw shellfish at a salad bar, cannot be offered for customer self-service.

Vending

Vending machines also fall in the category of self-service. Vending machine requirements include:

- Discarding any item past its use-by date;
- Keeping cold TCS foods at 41ºF (5ºC) or lower;
- Keeping hot TCS foods at 135ºF (57.2ºC) or higher;
- Washing and wrapping any foods with an edible peel; and
- Frequently checking the quality of items and discarding anything not fresh.

Serving Food Off-Site

Serving food off-site from where it was originally prepared has many of the same concerns as serving food on-site. Time/temperature abuse and cross-contamination must be avoided. This can be done by:

- Delivering foods in a clean, enclosed transport vehicle;
- Covering and protecting equipment such as insulated carrier carts and tray rack units;

- Transporting foods in clean containers that can maintain hot or cold temperatures;
- Labeling all food items;
- Having enough designated serving utensils;
- Wrapping utensils and enclosing them in containers; and
- Using time and temperature logs throughout the transport, delivery, and service.

Service Animals

Employees who come in contact with a **service animal** are required to wash their hands after each contact with the animal to remove bacteria and soil. Animals shed hair continuously and may deposit liquid or fecal waste, creating the need for vigilance and more frequent and rigorous cleaning efforts. A service animal is allowed in a food service or retail operation according to the Americans with Disabilities Act (ADA).

Chapter 9
Food Code Definitions

- **Re-service:** the transfer of food that is unused and returned by a consumer, after being served or sold and in the possession of the consumer, to another person.

- **Service animal:** an animal such as a guide dog, signal dog, or other animal specially trained to provide assistance to an individual with a disability.

Chapter 9
Conclusion

The PIC will need to ensure that foods being held for present or future use or service are maintained at safe temperatures. Foods that are being heated or cooled must be done under the proper time and temperature conditions to ensure that pathogens do not have the opportunity to grow. Foods that are being served or sold must be kept safe and away from contamination.

Chapter 9

Check for Understanding
(Circle one.)

1. Holding hot food on a serving line requires food to be held at a temperature of at least _____.

    a. 125°F (51.7°C)
    b. 130°F (54.4°C)
    c. 135°F (57.2°C)
    d. 140°F (60.0°C)

2. Holding chicken salad at a self-service buffet table requires a maximum holding temperature of _____.

    a. 55°F (12.7°C)
    b. 51°F (10.5°C)
    c. 45°F (7.2°C)
    d. 41°F (5.0°C)

3. When using time as a public health control for cold foods, the PIC must ensure that the food is _____.

    a. maintained at or below 70°F (21.1°C) at all times
    b. held at or above 70°F (21.1°C) at all times
    c. held up to eight hours
    d. maintained at or below 70°F (21.1°C) for up to six hours

4. The PIC must have self-service areas monitored to ensure that _____.

    a. the food is protected from contamination
    b. customers like the food
    c. food does not go to waste
    d. employees get enough hours

5. When catering foods off-site, the PIC must ensure that _____.

    a. all foods are labeled with their ingredients
    b. the off-site facility is supplied with appropriate handwashing facilities
    c. food temperatures are maintained during transport and holding before service
    d. all of the above

6. Cold TCS foods served out of a vending machine cannot exceed _____.

    a. 45°F (7.2°C)
    b. 32°F (0°C)
    c. 41°F (5.0°C)
    d. 70°F (21.1°C)

7. The sale of food from a self-service vending machine has specific requirements except _____.

  a. discarding any item passed its used-by date
  b. keeping cold TCS foods at 70°F (21.1°C) or lower
  c. keeping hot TCS foods at 135°F (57.2°C) or higher
  d. washing and wrapping any foods with an edible peel

8. Prepared food items sold or served to a customer can be returned for resale or re-service when the food is a _____.

  a. TCS food that is in its original sealed package
  b. TCS food returned with a receipt of purchase
  c. non-TCS food that is in its original sealed package
  d. non-TCS food that is removed from its original package but can be reused in making a cooked item with this food

9. The cooling process for hot TCS foods must be done by which method?

  a. 135°F (57.2°C) to 41°F (5.0°C) in five hours
  b. 135°F (57.2°C) to 70°F (21.1°C) within four hours, and 70°F (21.1°C) to 41°F (5.0°C) in an additional four hours
  c. 135°F (57.2°C) to 41°F (5.0°C) in six hours
  d. 135°F (57.2°C) to 70°F (21.1°C) within two hours, and 70°F (21.1°C) to 41°F (5.0°C) in an additional four hours

10. Acceptable cooling techniques include using all except _____.

  a. ice as an ingredient for a cooked food that needs to be cooled
  b. an ice paddle to stir hot liquid foods
  c. a freezer to cool the food
  d. shallow pans in a blast chiller

FDA Food Code References

Chapter 3 – Food

- 3-4 Destruction of Organisms of Public Health Concern
    - 3-403.10 Preparation for Immediate Service
    - 3-403.11 Reheating for Hot Holding
- 3-5 Limitation of Growth of Organisms of Public Health Concern
    - 3-501.14 Cooling
    - 3-501.15 Cooling Methods
    - 3-501.16 Time/Temperature Control for Safety Food, Hot and Cold Holding
    - 3-501.19 Time as a Public Health Control

Chapter 6 – Physical Facilities

- 6-5 Maintenance and Operation
    - 6-501.115 Prohibiting Animals

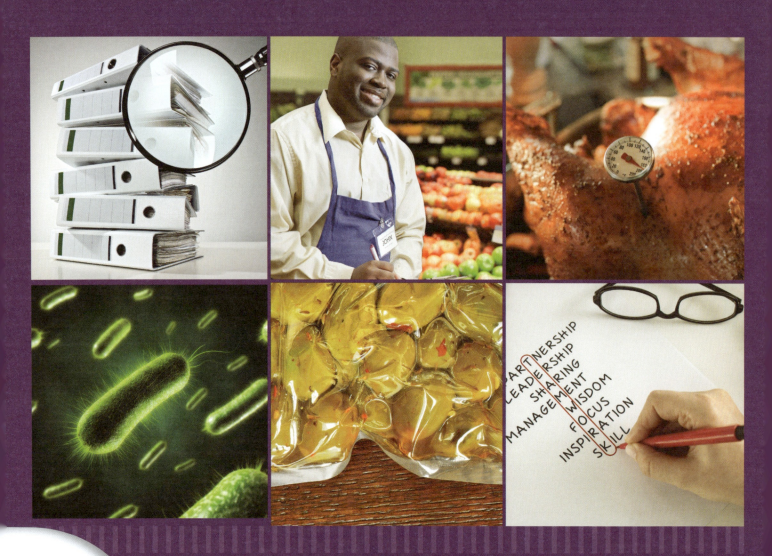

Chapter 10:
Applying HACCP to Food Service and Retail Establishments

Chapter 10: Goals

In this chapter, participants will learn to:

- Define HACCP and the seven HACCP principles.
- Identify when a HACCP plan is required.
- Recognize the PIC's responsibilities with regards to HACCP.
- Apply the seven HACCP principles to a food service or retail establishment.

Chapter 10: Myth or Fact

(Check one.)

1. A critical control point is any step in the flow of food where a hazard can be controlled.
   ✓ Myth ___ Fact

2. A critical limit is a maximum or minimum specific boundary required for each critical control point.
   ___ Myth ✓ Fact

3. A HACCP plan is a written document that a food service or retail establishment must follow if a specialty process is used and a variance is granted.
   ___ Myth ✓ Fact

4. HACCP analyzes biological, chemical, and radiological hazards that may cause an unacceptable health risk.
   ✓ Myth ___ Fact

5. A variance is a written document issued by the regulatory authority that authorizes an exception to the Food Code.
   ___ Myth ✓ Fact

HACCP Overview

HACCP stands for Hazard Analysis and Critical Control Point. A **HACCP plan** is a written document that assesses hazards in an operation and identifies ways to prevent, eliminate, and reduce the hazards to safe levels. It is a systematic approach used to limit the risk when serving or selling food. HACCP is a common practice used in food manufacturing and processing plants, as well as in schools that receive federal funding. HACCP is mandated by regulatory authorities when specialized processing methods are used and/or when a variance is required. **Variance** means a written document issued by the regulatory authority that authorizes a modification or waiver of one or more requirements of the Food Code if, in the opinion of the regulatory authority, a health hazard or nuisance will not result from the modification or waiver.

A variance is required when the following specialized processes are used:

- Smoking food for preservation;
- Curing food;
- Using food additives for preservation;
- Operating a specialized life support system for shellfish;
- Custom processing animals;
- Sprouting seeds or beans;
- Packaging juice to be served later;
- Packaging certain foods that do not control for the growth of *Clostridium botulinum* and *Listeria monocytogenes* with Reduced Oxygen Packaging (ROP) methods;
    - Sous vide
    - Vacuum packed
    - Modified Atmosphere Packaging (MAP)
    - Controlled Atmosphere Packaging (CAP)
    - Cook-Chill
- Another method requiring an exception to the Food Code.

Reduced Oxygen Packaging (ROP) Methods

Sous vide (SV): cold food is packed with ROP and cooked in the sealed package before sale or service.

Cook-Chill (CC): cooked food is packed with ROP and then cooled.

Vacuum packed (VP): food is placed in a package from which the air is removed, and the package is sealed.

Modified Atmosphere Packaging (MAP): process in which a gas is introduced into the package to replace oxygen.

Controlled Atmosphere Packaging (CAP): process in which an agent is introduced into the package to maintain a specific oxygen level.

When using the specialized processes, there is an added concern for public health hazards. A request for a variance may require:

1. A statement about the Food Code requirement that needs to be modified;

2. Detailed explanations for how potential public health hazards will be addressed with the modification;

3. A HACCP plan; and

4. A training plan that addresses the food safety issues of concern.

HACCP plans are needed to protect the establishment and its customers from risks and illnesses, as well as create a reasonable care defense. The PIC needs to assemble a HACCP team to develop and implement a customized HACCP plan for their food service or retail operation. The HACCP team should include anyone with key responsibilities in the operation who can contribute their area of expertise to the plan.

There are many factors that can affect the hazards and the plan. When developing a HACCP plan, the team must take into account the following factors:

- Customer base (general or highly susceptible populations);
- Employee qualifications (knowledge, skills, and ability);
- Facility design (layout, equipment, and capacity);
- Intended use of the food (purchase and prepare at home, immediate consumption, or partially cooked);
- Concept (food products, recipes, and ingredients); and
- A process approach (Simple/No-Cook, Same-Day, and Complex).

All of these elements impact the HACCP plan as far as determining the hazards (biological, chemical, and physical) and how they can be prevented, eliminated, or reduced to safe levels. In food service and retail establishments, the number of food products can be overwhelming, and this factor must be managed. When creating a HACCP plan, there is an easy way to manage the large number of food products. The food products can be simply divided into Simple/No-Cook, Same-Day, and Complex categories. The categories are based on the number of times a food product moves through the temperature danger zone (TDZ) as shown in the following graph.

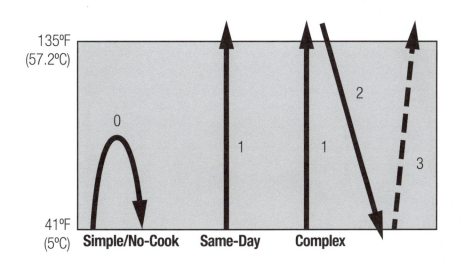

Pop Quiz:

Food Product Categories
(Check one.)

Identify the following food items as Simple/No-Cook, Same-Day, or Complex.

1. In the meat department of a grocery store, raw beef, pork, and lamb roasts are available for purchase by their customers.
   ___Simple/No-Cook   ___Same-Day   ___Complex

2. A food service operation is preparing potato salad with hard boiled eggs in the recipe.
   ___Simple/No-Cook   ___Same-Day   ___Complex

3. A convenience store is stocking pre-made tuna salad sandwiches.
   ___Simple/No-Cook   ___Same-Day   ___Complex

4. A restaurant is cooking lobster tail for an elderly person.
   ___Simple/No-Cook   ___Same-Day   ___Complex

5. A retail operation is selling whole roasted chicken.
   ___Simple/No-Cook   ___Same-Day   ___Complex

The seven HACCP principles are:

1. Conduct a hazard analysis
2. Determine critical control points
3. Establish critical limits
4. Establish monitoring procedures
5. Establish corrective actions
6. Verification
7. Record keeping and documentation

HACCP Principle 1: Conduct a Hazard Analysis

The first HACCP principle is to conduct a hazard analysis. **Hazard** refers to a biological, chemical, or physical property that may cause an unacceptable consumer health risk. This principle identifies any potential hazards in the food. It takes into consideration the concept, process steps, food items, ingredients, and the flow of food. This analysis determines if any of the food items or ingredients are a TCS food. When a TCS food is identified, then the biological, chemical, or physical hazards must be determined.

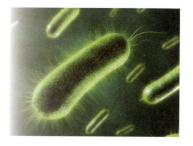

Example

A menu has two items on it: soft drinks and hamburgers. The TCS food is identified as a hamburger. The hazard associated with a hamburger would be *E. coli* O157:H7 in ground beef, which is a biological hazard.

HACCP Principle 2: Determine Critical Control Points

Every food item follows a specific flow of food, and all control points and critical control points must be documented at each step. A **control point** is any step in the flow of food when control can be applied to prevent, eliminate, and reduce biological, chemical, or physical hazards. A **critical control point (CCP)** is a point or procedure in a specific food system where loss of control may result in an unacceptable health risk. A CCP is an operational step, point, or procedure at which control can be applied and is essential to prevent, eliminate, or reduce a hazard to an acceptable level.

This is often the last step in the flow of food before the food is sold or served. However, in a retail setting, it may be one of the first steps. Keep in mind that there may be multiple CCPs.

Determining the CCP will depend on the product selected. Here are some questions to consider when determining the CCP:

- Is the food item raw or RTE?
- Is there a preparation step?
- Does the food item need further assembly?
- Are other ingredients introduced into the product?

Example

The meat is a frozen, formed, raw ground beef patty. The flow of food for the hamburger is: receive, store, cook, hot hold, and serve. Each step is identified as either a CP or a CCP.

- **Receive – CP**
- **Store – CP**
- **Cook – CCP**
- **Hot Hold – CCP**
- **Serve**

HACCP Principle 3: Establish Critical Limits

Each CCP will have a critical limit, a measurable and specific boundary based on scientific measures. A **critical limit** is the maximum or minimum value to which a physical, biological, or chemical parameter must be controlled at a critical control point to minimize the risk that the identified food safety hazard may occur.

The critical limit must be met in order to prevent, eliminate, or reduce the hazard to a safe level. Critical limits can be time, temperature, water activity, or acidity. The critical limit will vary based on the product, type of food, ingredients used, and recipe.

Example

CCP	CL
Cooking	155ºF (68.3ºC) for 15 seconds
Hot holding	135ºF (57.2ºC)

- Cooking is the CCP, and the critical limit is 155ºF (68.3ºC) for 15 seconds.
- Hot holding is the CCP, and the critical limit is 135ºF (57.2ºC).

HACCP Principle 4: Establish Monitoring Procedures

Monitoring is essential for ensuring that the critical limit for each CCP has been reached. This could be accomplished using continuous or non-continuous monitoring. **Continuous monitoring** allows for constant measurement of the CCP. This is usually done by an automated system. **Non-continuous monitoring** occurs at specific times, intervals, or per batch. Non-continuous is often a manual testing process. In the HACCP plan it must be predetermined how and when monitoring will be conducted, as well as who will be monitoring.

Example

Each hamburger is checked by the chef using non-continuous monitoring with a calibrated, cleaned, and sanitized thermometer.

HACCP Principle 5: Establish Corrective Actions

When monitoring, if it is observed that the critical limit has not been met, then immediate action must be taken, which is a **corrective action**. This is predetermined based on the HACCP plan. Corrective actions could include:

- Continue to cook;
- Reheat;
- Discard;
- Cool;
- Retrain;
- Recalibrate; and
- Reject.

Example

The chef checks the hamburger's internal product temperature and it reads 143°F (61.6°C). The chef immediately takes corrective action and continues to cook the hamburger until it reaches the critical limit of 155°F (68.3°C) for 15 seconds. The critical limit must be met in order to eliminate the potential *E. coli* O157:H7 in the hamburger. The chef monitored the internal product temperature of the hamburger, and at the next temperature check, he recorded the hamburger temperature at 157°F (69.4°C). The chef then documented this temperature on the proper form.

HACCP Principle 6: Verification

Verification is accomplished by making sure that monitoring was completed, critical limits were met, and the hazards have been prevented, eliminated, or reduced to safe levels. This is done in order to confirm that the HACCP plan is being followed. The person who monitors cannot carry out the verification process. Verification may be done by supervisors, managers, directors, or an outside firm.

Example

The PIC verified that the HACCP plan was working as intended by observing the chef monitoring the hamburger and reviewing the temperature logs.

Chapter 10 | Page 143

HACCP Principle 7: Record Keeping and Documentation

Documentation is important because it shows that the HACCP plan has been carried out as intended. Typical HACCP plan documentation includes: Hazard Analysis Worksheet, flow diagrams, recipes, standard operating procedures, monitoring records, and the HACCP plan. Record keeping also provides the documentation for a reasonable care defense.

Example

The following records were used in the operation and maintained in the PIC's office:

- Purchasing specifications provided to the supplier;
- Invoice used at receiving to document the receiving temperature;
- Refrigerated Storage Continuous Monitoring Log (automatically recorded every 15 minutes);
- Cooking Log;
- Hot Holding Log;
- Corrective Action Log; and
- Serving Log.

Pop Quiz:

HACCP
(Complete.)

What does each letter represent in the acronym HACCP?

1. H = _____

2. A = _____

3. C = _____

4. C = _____

5. P = _____

Chapter 10
Food Code Definitions

- **Controlled Atmosphere Packaging (CAP):** process in which an agent is introduced into the package to maintain a specific oxygen level.

- **Cook-Chill (CC):** cooked food is packed with ROP, and then cooled.

- **Critical control point:** a point or procedure in a specific food system where loss of control may result in an unacceptable health risk.

- **Critical limit:** the maximum or minimum value to which a physical, biological, or chemical parameter must be controlled at a critical control point to minimize the risk that the identified food safety hazard may occur.

- **HACCP plan:** a written document that assesses hazards in an operation and finds ways to prevent, eliminate, and reduce the hazards to safe levels.

- **Hazard:** a biological, chemical, or physical property that may cause an unacceptable consumer health risk.

- **Modified Atmosphere Packaging (MAP):** process in which a gas is introduced into the package to replace oxygen.

- **Sous vide (SV):** cold food is packed with ROP and cooked in the sealed package before sale or service.

- **Vacuum packed (VP):** food is placed in a package from which the air is removed, and the package is sealed.

- **Variance:** a written document issued by the regulatory authority that authorizes a modification or waiver of one or more requirements of the Food Code if, in the opinion of the regulatory authority, a health hazard or nuisance will not result from the modification or waiver.

Chapter 10
Conclusion

In Chapter 10, HACCP is defined and the seven HACCP principles are applied to a food service or retail facility. The PIC has responsibilities that must be performed in terms of implementing a HACCP plan. A HACCP plan is required for obtaining a variance to conduct specific food handling processes. As an example, a high risk process requiring a variance is packaging food using a ROP method with the hazards of *Clostridium botulinum* and *Listeria monocytogenes* that must be prevented, eliminated, or reduced by the HACCP plan.

Chapter 10

Check for Understanding

(Circle one.)

1. A variance from a regulatory authority to modify or waive a particular food handling or food processing restriction can include the following except _____.
    a. smoking meat or fish to preserve it
    b. using spices in the preparation of foods
    c. reducing the oxygen environment of food
    d. sprouting seeds or beans to serve or sell to customers

2. Several methods of reducing the oxygen environment of food can be used. Which method does not require regulatory variance approval?
    a. Producing cook-chill processed foods
    b. Producing sous vide processed foods
    c. Producing vacuum packaged foods
    d. Producing foil-wrapped baked potatoes

3. An employee cooks chicken to 165ºF (73.5ºC) for 15 seconds. Cooking the chicken is the _____.
    a. hazard analysis
    b. corrective action
    ~~c. critical limit~~
    d. critical control point

4. Food handling processes can be categorized into three types, which include _____.
    a. 1 - Complex   2 - Same-Day   3 - Simple
    b. 1 - Same Day   2 - Simple/No-Cook   3 - Complex
    c. 1 - Simple/No-Cook   2 - Same-Day   3 - Complex   — 139
    d. 1 - Simple/Same Day 2 - No-Cook   3 - Complex

5. A CCP for Simple/No-Cook tuna salad made on-site would be _____.
    a. purchase
    b. receive
    c. prepare
    d. cold holding

6. An example of a corrective action is _____.
   a. purchasing a product
   b. hiring a new chef
   c. reheating a product
   d. serving undercooked food

7. Establishing a critical limit is a HACCP principle that requires identifying _____.
   a. the step in a process when not controlled will result is an unsafe product
   b. the measurement that has to be taken and the specific value of the measurement to achieve
   c. the measurement that has to be taken at each step in the food preparation process
   d. the measurement of correction steps that need to be taken to produce a safe food

8. HACCP Plan documents such as cooking logs, invoices, and training records are part of which principle?
   a. Record keeping and documentation
   b. Establish monitoring procedures
   c. Establish critical limits
   d. Conduct a hazard analysis

9. Some of the HACCP principles are establishing _____.
   a. critical limits, control points, and control procedures
   b. critical control points, corrections, and limits
   c. critical control points, corrective actions, and critical limits
   d. control limits, corrective actions, and conducting a hazard analysis

10. Which of the following is an example of a critical limit?
   a. Minimum internal cooking temperature of 155°F (68.3°C) for 15 seconds
   b. Sushi rice pH below 4.6
   c. Reheating food to 165°F (73.9°C) for 15 seconds within 2 hours
   d. All of the above

FDA Food Code References

Variances and Specialized Processing Methods
Chapter 3 – Food
- 3-5 Limitation of Growth of Organisms of Public Health Concern
    - 3-502.11 Variance Requirement

Chapter 8 – Compliance & Enforcement
- 8-1 Code Applicability
    - 8-103.10 Modifications and Waivers
    - 8-103.11 Documentation of Proposed Variance and Justification
    - 8-103.12 Conformance with Approved Procedures

Answer Key

Food Safety Pre-Test (Pages 3-5)
1. d
2. a
3. d
4. c
5. c
6. d
7. c
8. a
9. d
10. c
11. d
12. c
13. c
14. b
15. d
16. b
17. c
18. a
19. c
20. d

Chapter 1

Myth or Fact (Page 9)
1. Myth
2. Fact
3. Myth
4. Fact
5. Myth

Pop Quiz: Food Defense (Page 12)
1. Assure
2. Look
3. Employees
4. Reports
5. Threats

Pop Quiz: Person-in-Charge (Page 15)
1. Yes
2. No
3. Yes
4. Yes
5. No

Check for Understanding (Pages 18-19)
1. d
2. a
3. b
4. c
5. d
6. c
7. d
8. d
9. c
10. d

Chapter 2

Myth or Fact (Page 21)
1. Myth
2. Myth
3. Myth
4. Fact
5. Myth

Pop Quiz: Highly Susceptible Populations (Page 24)
1. Yes
2. Yes
3. Yes
4. Yes
5. No

Pop Quiz: FATTOM (Page 26)
Check: 1, 2, 5, 7, 9, 10

Check for Understanding (Pages 33-34)
1. a
2. c
3. c
4. c
5. b
6. b
7. c
8. d
9. b
10. c

Chapter 3

Myth or Fact (Page 37)
1. Fact
2. Myth
3. Fact
4. Fact
5. Fact

Pop Quiz: Bacteria (Page 41)
1. d
2. e
3. c
4. b
5. a

Pop Quiz: PIC Managing Microorganisms (Page 44)
1. Yes
2. Yes
3. No
4. No
5. Yes

Check for Understanding (Pages 46-47)
1. c
2. c
3. a
4. c
5. b
6. d
7. b
8. a
9. a
10. c

Chapter 4

Myth or Fact (Page 49)

1. Myth
2. Myth
3. Fact
4. Myth
5. Fact

Pop Quiz: Facilities by the Numbers (Page 55)

1. one, one
2. 100ºF (37.8ºC)
3. 6 inches (15 cm)
4. one
5. 4 inches (10 cm)

Pop Quiz: Waste and Water (Page 59)

1. No
2. Yes
3. No
4. No
5. Yes

Check for Understanding (Pages 61-62)

1. b
2. d
3. c
4. c
5. a
6. d
7. c
8. c
9. d
10. c

Chapter 5

Myth or Fact (Page 65)

1. Myth
2. Fact
3. Myth
4. Myth
5. Fact

Pop Quiz: Cleaning by the Numbers (Page 72)

1. 110ºF (43.3ºC)
2. 75ºF (23.9ºC)
3. 4
4. 6 inches (15 cm)
5. 171ºF (77.2ºC)

Pop Quiz: Chemicals and Pests (Page 75)

1. No
2. No
3. No
4. No
5. Yes

Check for Understanding (Pages 77-78)

1. c
2. b
3. b
4. d
5. c
6. c
7. b
8. d
9. d
10. c

Chapter 6

Myth or Fact (Page 81)

1. Myth
2. Fact
3. Myth
4. Fact
5. Myth

Pop Quiz: Handwashing (Page 85)

1. After
2. Before
3. After
4. After
5. After
6. Before
7. Before, After
8. Before
9. After
10. After
11. After
12. After
13. After
14. Before
15. After

Pop Quiz: Employee Health (Page 90)

Check: 2, 5, 8, 10

Check for Understanding (Pages 92-93)

1. a
2. b
3. d
4. a
5. c
6. c
7. d
8. b
9. b
10. d

Chapter 7

Myth or Fact (Page 97)

1. Myth
2. Myth
3. Fact
4. Myth
5. Myth

Pop Quiz: Receiving and Storing (Page 103)

1. No
2. No
3. No
4. Yes
5. Yes

Pop Quiz: Food Labeling (Page 106)
1. Yes
2. No
3. Yes
4. No
5. No

Check for Understanding
(Pages 108-109)
1. c
2. d
3. a
4. b
5. b
6. c
7. b
8. c
9. a
10. b

Chapter 8
Myth or Fact (Page 113)
1. Myth
2. Myth
3. Fact
4. Fact
5. Fact

Pop Quiz: Safe Food (Page 117)
1. No
2. No
3. Yes
4. No
5. No
6. No
7. Yes
8. No
9. No
10. Yes

Pop Quiz: Safe Food Overview
(Page 120)
1. No
2. Yes
3. No
4. No
5. No

Check for Understanding
(Pages 122-123)
1. d
2. c
3. b
4. c
5. b
6. a
7. d
8. d
9. d
10. b

Chapter 9
Myth or Fact (Page 125)
1. Fact
2. Myth
3. Myth
4. Myth
5. Fact

Pop Quiz: Temperatures (Page 128)
1. d
2. c
3. a
4. e
5. b

Pop Quiz: Service (Page 130)
1. Yes
2. Yes
3. No
4. No
5. Yes

Check for Understanding
(Pages 133-134)
1. c
2. d
3. d
4. a
5. d
6. c
7. b
8. c
9. d
10. c

Chapter 10
Myth or Fact (Page 137)
1. Myth
2. Fact
3. Fact
4. Myth
5. Fact

Pop Quiz: Food Product Categories
(Page 140)
1. Simple/No-Cook
2. Complex
3. Simple/No-Cook
4. Same-Day
5. Same-Day

Pop Quiz: HACCP (Page 144)
1. Hazard
2. Analysis
3. Critical
4. Control
5. Point

Check for Understanding
(Pages 146-147)
1. b
2. d
3. d
4. c
5. d
6. c
7. b
8. a
9. c
10. d

Glossary

A

Active managerial control – a proactive food safety management system that creates procedures to control the CDC risk factors

Air gap – the physical separation of air between the water supply and plumbing equipment

Asymptomatic – without obvious symptoms; not showing or producing indications of a disease or other medical condition, such as an individual infected with a pathogen but not exhibiting or producing any signs or symptoms of vomiting, diarrhea, or jaundice. Asymptomatic includes not showing symptoms because symptoms have resolved or subsided, or because symptoms never manifested.

a_w (water activity) – a measure of the free moisture in a food, is the quotient of the water vapor pressure of the substance divided by the vapor pressure of pure water at the same temperature

B

Backflow – occurs when negative pressure creates back siphonage, which causes contamination of the water system

Bacteria – unicellular microorganisms that can grow in people and in food

Balut – an embryo inside a fertile egg that has been incubated for a period sufficient for the embryo to reach a specific stage of development, after which it is removed from incubation before hatching

Biological hazards – harmful microorganisms known as pathogens that include viruses, bacteria, fungi, and parasites

C

Chemical hazards – substances that are naturally occurring or added to foods that can cause illness or injury when consumed

Cleaning – process to remove dirt and other contaminates from a surface

Comminuted – reduced in size by methods including chopping, flaking, grinding, or mincing. Comminuted includes fish or meat products that are reduced in size and restructured or reformulated such as gefilte fish, gyros, ground beef, and sausage; and a mixture of two or more types of meat that has been reduced in size and combined, such as sausages made from two or more meats.

Conditional employee – a potential food employee to whom a job offer is made, conditional on responses to subsequent medical questions or examinations designed to identify potential food employees who may be suffering from a disease that can be transmitted through food and done in compliance with Title 1 of the Americans with Disabilities Act of 1990

Confirmed disease outbreak – a foodborne disease outbreak in which laboratory analysis of appropriate specimens identifies a causative agent, and epidemiological analysis implicates the food as the source of the illness

Continuous monitoring – constant measurement

Control point – any step in the flow of food when control can be applied to prevent, eliminate, or reduce biological, chemical, or physical hazards

Controlled Atmosphere Packaging (CAP) – process in which an agent is introduced into the package to maintain a specific oxygen level.

Cook-Chill (CC) – cooked food is packed with reduced oxygen packaging, and then cooled

Cooling – process done when food hot from being cooked or heated, or warm from being handled and prepared, that needs to be cold for holding and future use is reduced in temperature to below 41°F (5°C) for food safety

Core food safety features – the physical components of the establishment's premise related to a safe water supply, plumbing system, sanitation and cleanliness, food equipment placement, food equipment cleaning, physical conditions, item storage, and facilities to ensure employee hygiene

Corrective action – immediate action taken when a critical limit is not met

Critical control point – a point or procedure in a specific food system where loss of control may result in an unacceptable health risk

Critical limit – the maximum or minimum value to which a physical, biological, or chemical parameter must be controlled at a critical control point to minimize the risk that the identified food safety hazard may occur

Cross-contact – when an allergen transfers from one food or surface to another

Cross-contamination – occurs when pathogens transfer from one food surface to another.

D

Data plate – warewashing machine operating specifications affixed to the machine

Disclosure – a written statement that clearly identifies the animal-derived foods which are, or can be ordered, raw, undercooked, or without otherwise being processed to eliminate pathogens, or items that contain an ingredient that is raw, undercooked, or without otherwise being processed to eliminate pathogens

E

Employee – the permit holder, person-in-charge, food employee, person having supervisory or management duties, person on the payroll, family member, volunteer, person performing work under contractual agreement, or other person working in a food establishment

F

FDA – United States Food and Drug Administration

Fish – fresh or saltwater finfish, crustaceans and other forms of aquatic life (including alligator, frog, aquatic turtle, jellyfish, sea cucumber, and sea urchin and the roe of such animals) other than birds or mammals, and all mollusks, if such animal life is intended for human consumption. Fish includes an edible human food product derived in whole or in part from fish, including fish that have been processed in any manner.

Food – a raw, cooked, or processed edible substance, ice, beverage, or ingredient used or intended for use or for sale in whole or in part for human consumption, or chewing gum

Food-contact surface – (1) A surface of equipment or a utensil with which food normally comes into contact; or (2) a surface of equipment or a utensil from which food may drain, drip, or splash: (a) into a food, or (b) onto a surface normally in contact with food

Foodborne disease outbreak – the occurrence of two or more cases of a similar illness resulting from the ingestion of a common food

Foodborne illness – a sickness that results from the consumption of food or beverages contaminated with disease-causing microorganisms, chemicals, or other harmful substances

Food Code – a model document for safeguarding public health and ensuring that food is safe when offered to consumers. The Food Code is a guidance document that contains practical, science-based information and provisions for mitigating risk factors known to cause foodborne illness.

Food defense – the act of preventing an intentional contamination of food

Food employee – an individual working with unpackaged food, food equipment or utensils, or food-contact surfaces

Food establishment – an operation that (a) stores, prepares, packages, serves, vends food directly to the consumer, or otherwise provides food for human consumption such as a restaurant; satellite or catered feeding location; catering operation if the operation provides food directly to a consumer or to a conveyance used to transport people; market; vending location; conveyance used to transport people; institution; or food bank; and (b) relinquishes possession of food to a consumer directly, or indirectly through a delivery service such as home delivery of grocery orders or restaurant takeout orders, or delivery service that is provided by common carriers

Food safety – the protection from unintentional contamination of food

Fungi – spoilage microorganisms, including molds, yeasts, and mushrooms

G

Game animal – an animal, the products of which are food, that is not classified as livestock, sheep, swine, goat, horse, mule, or other equine in 9 CFR 301.2 Definitions, or as poultry, or fish. Game animals include mammals such as reindeer, elk, deer, antelope, water buffalo, bison, rabbit, squirrel, opossum, raccoon, nutria, or muskrat, and nonaquatic reptiles such as land snakes. Game animals do not include ratites.

Grade A standard – the requirements of the United States Public Health Service/FDA "Grade A Pasteurized Milk Ordinance" with which certain fluid and dry milk and milk products comply

H

HACCP – Hazard Analysis and Critical Control Point

HACCP plan – a written document that assesses hazards in an operation and finds ways to prevent, eliminate, and reduce the hazards to safe levels

Handwashing sink – a lavatory, a basin or vessel for washing, a wash basin, or a plumbing fixture especially placed for use in personal hygiene and designed for the washing of the hands. It also includes an automatic handwashing facility.

Hazard – a biological, chemical, or physical property that may cause an unacceptable consumer health risk

Highly susceptible population – persons who are more likely than other people in the general population to experience foodborne disease because they are: (1) Immunocompromised; preschool-aged children, or older adults; and (2) Obtaining food at a facility that provides services such as custodial care, health care, or assisted living, such as a child or adult day care center, kidney dialysis center, hospital or nursing home, or nutritional or socialization services such as a senior center

I

Imminent health hazard – a significant threat or danger to health

Infection – microorganism enters the body and grows, causing illness

Intoxication or poisoning – microorganism-created toxin, a toxic or poisonous substance, that when ingested causes illness

J

Juice – the aqueous liquid expressed or extracted from one or more fruits or vegetables, purées of the edible portions of one or more fruits or vegetables, or any concentrates of such liquid or purée

M

Major food allergen – (a) Milk, eggs, fish (such as bass, flounder, and cod, and including crustacean shellfish such as crab, lobster, or shrimp), tree nuts (such as almonds, pecans, or walnuts), wheat, peanuts, and soybeans; or (b) A food ingredient that contains protein derived from a food, as specified in (a) of this definition

Meat – the flesh of animals used as food including the dressed flesh of cattle, wine, sheep, or goats and other edible animals, except fish, poultry, and wild game animals

Mechanically tenderized – manipulating meat with deep penetration by processes that may be referred to as "blade tenderizing," "jaccarding," "pinning," "needling," or using blades, pins, needles or any mechanical device. Mechanically tenderized does not include processes by which solutions are injected into meat.

Modified Atmosphere Packaging (MAP) – process in which a gas is introduced into the package to replace oxygen

Molluscan shellfish – an edible species of fresh or frozen oysters, clams, mussels, and scallops or edible portions thereof, except when the scallop product consists only of the shucked adductor muscle

N

Non-continuous cooking – the cooking of food in a food establishment using a process in which the initial heating of the food is intentionally halted so that it may be cooled and held for complete cooking at a later time prior to sale or service. Non-continuous cooking does not include cooking procedures that only involve temporarily interrupting or slowing an otherwise continuous cooking process.

Non-continuous monitoring – measurement that occurs at specific times, intervals, or per batch

P

Packaged – bottled, canned, cartooned, bagged, or wrapped, whether packed in a food establishment or a food processing plant

Parasite – an organism that lives on or in a host organism and gets its food from, or at the expense of, its host

Person-in-charge (PIC) – the individual present at a food establishment who is responsible for the operation at the time of inspection

Personal care items – items or substances that may be poisonous, toxic, or a source of contamination and are used to maintain or enhance a person's health, hygiene, or appearance. These include items such as medicines, first-aid supplies, and other items such as cosmetics, and toiletries such as toothpaste and mouthwash.

pH – the symbol for the negative logarithm of the hydrogen ion concentration, which is a measure of the degree of acidity or alkalinity of a solution. Values between 0 and 7 indicate acidity, and values between 7 and 14 indicate alkalinity. The value for pure distilled water is 7, which is considered neutral.

Physical hazards – foreign objects not expected to be in food that can cause harm to the consumer

Plumbing systems – designed and installed to ensure safety of the water supply

Poisonous or toxic materials – substances that are not intended for ingestion and fall within four categories:(1) cleaners and sanitizers, which include cleaning and sanitizing agents and agents such as caustics, acids, drying agents, polishes, and other chemicals; (2) pesticides, except sanitizers, which include substances such as insecticides and rodenticides; (3) substances necessary for the operation and maintenance of the establishment such as nonfood-grade lubricants and personal care items that may be deleterious to health; and (4) substances that are not necessary for the operation and maintenance of the establishment and are on the premises for retail sale, such as petroleum products and paints

Potable water – water used for drinking and food preparation

Poultry – any domesticated bird (chickens, turkeys, ducks, geese, guineas, ratites, or squabs), whether live or dead, as defined in 9 CFR 381.1 Poultry Products Inspection Regulations Definitions, Poultry; and any migratory waterfowl or game bird, pheasant, partridge, quail, grouse, or pigeon, whether live or dead, as defined in 9 CFR 362.1 Voluntary Poultry Inspection Regulations Definitions

Premises – (1) The physical facility, its contents, and the contiguous land or property under the control of the permit holder; or (2) the physical facility, its contents, and the land or property not described in subparagraph (1) of this definition if its facilities and contents are under the control of the permit holder and may impact food establishment personnel, facilities, or operations, and a food establishment is only one component of a larger operation such as a health care facility, hotel, motel, school, recreational camp, or prison

R

Ratite – a flightless bird such as an emu, ostrich, or rhea

Re-service – the transfer of food that is unused and returned by a consumer, after being served or sold and in the possession of the consumer, to another person

Ready-to-eat (RTE) food – food that is edible without additional preparation

Reminder – a written statement concerning the health risk of consuming animal foods raw, undercooked, or without otherwise being processed to eliminate pathogens

Restrict – to limit the activities of a food employee so that there is no risk of transmitting a disease that is transmissible through food and so that the food employee does not work with exposed food, clean equipment, utensils, linens, or unwrapped single-service or single-use articles

Risk – the likelihood that an adverse health effect will occur within a population as a result of a hazard in a food

S

Sanitization – the application of cumulative heat or chemicals on cleaned food-contact surfaces that, when evaluated for efficacy, is sufficient to yield a reduction of 5 logs, which is equal to a 99.999% reduction, of representative disease microorganisms of public health importance

Sanitizing – process to reduce pathogens to a safe level on a clean surface

Service animal – an animal such as a guide dog, signal dog, or other animal specially trained to provide assistance to an individual with a disability

Shellstock – raw, in-shell molluscan shellfish

Shucked shellfish – molluscan shellfish that have one or both shells removed

Slacking – the processes of moderating the temperature of a food, such as allowing a food to gradually increase from a temperature of -10°F – 25°F (-23°C – -4°C) in preparation for deep-fat frying or to facilitate even heat penetration during the cooking of previously block-frozen food such as shrimp

Sous vide (SV) – cold food is packed with reduced oxygen packaging and cooked in the sealed package before sale or service

T

Time as a public health control – holding food without using equipment to maintain temperatures using time as the means of ensuring food safety

Time temperature abuse – food remains in the temperature danger zone of 41°F – 135°F (5°C – 57.2°C) for too long

Time/temperature control for safety (TCS) foods – foods that cannot be in the temperature danger zone for certain amounts of time to prevent pathogenic microorganism growth or toxin formation

Toxin-mediated infection – microorganism in the body producing a toxin that causes illness

U

USDA – United States Department of Agriculture

Utensil – a food-contact implement or container used in the storage, preparation, transportation, dispensing, sale, or service of food, such as kitchenware or tableware that is multiuse, single-service, or single-use; gloves used in contact with food; temperature-sensing probes of food temperature measuring devices; and probe-type price or identification tags used in contact with food

V

Vacuum packed (VP) – food is placed in a package from which the air is removed, and the package is sealed

Variance – a written document issued by the regulatory authority that authorizes a modification or waiver of one or more requirements of the Food Code if, in the opinion of the regulatory authority, a health hazard or nuisance will not result from the modification or waiver

Ventilation systems – circulates air to keep operations free of excessive heat, steam, condensation, vapors, obnoxious odors, and smoke

Verification – confirming a HACCP plan was followed properly

Viruses – smallest of the pathogens and can only be replicated inside living cells or an organism

W

Warewashing – the cleaning and sanitizing of utensils and food-contact surfaces of equipment

Whole-muscle, intact beef – whole-muscle beef that is not injected, mechanically tenderized, reconstructed, or scored and marinated, from which beef steaks may be cut

Index

A

Acidity
    Acidity and FATTOM, 25-26
    Acidity, *see also* pH
Active managerial control
    Active managerial control implementing, 15
    Active managerial control addressing the risk factors, 15, 45, 66, 82, 98, 114, 126
    Active managerial control defined, 152
    Active Managerial Control Used to Control Microorganisms, 45
Air gap, 58, 152
Allergens
    Allergens and assisting customers, 31
    Allergens as chemical hazards, 22
    Allergens associated with food preparation, 31
    Allergens Big 8, 30
    Allergens defined, 30
    Allergens and packaged food, 30
    Allergens and reactions, 30
    Allergens and serving food, 31, 129
    Allergens and symptoms, 30
    Allergens *see also* Food allergies
American National Standards Institute (ANSI), 51
Amnesic shellfish poisoning (ASP), 43, 45
Anaphylaxis, 30
Anisakiasis, 42
Anisakis simplex, 42
ANSI, *see* American National Standards Institute
Approved source
    Approved source, defined, 98
    Approved source and potable water, 57-58
    Approved source and purchasing food, 22, 42
ASP (amnesic shellfish poisoning), 43, 45
Asymptomatic, 43, 45, 152
a_w, *see* Water activity

B

Bacillus cereus, 40-41
Backflow, 58, 152
Bacteria
    Bacteria as biological hazards, 22, 38
    Bacteria barriers that prohibit growth of, 25, 40
    Bacteria defined, 40, 152
    Bacteria sources, 40-41, 82-83, 100, 105, 132
Balut, 114, 120, 152
Big 6 foodborne illnesses, 10, 87
Big 8 food allergens, 30
Biological hazards
    Biological hazards as most common hazard, 22, 38
    Biological hazards and control, 25, 38
    Biological hazards defined, 22, 38 152
    Biological hazards example of, 141
Boiling-point calibrating thermometers, 29
Bones (as physical hazards), 23
Botulism, 40

C

Calibration of thermometers, 28-29
Campylobacter jejuni, 40, 88
CAP foods, *see* controlled atmosphere packing foods
CC, *see* Cook-chill processing
CCP, *see* Critical control point
CDC, *see* Center for Disease Control and Prevention
Centers for Disease Control and Prevention (CDC)
    Centers for Disease Control and Prevention (CDC) estimated foodborne illnesses, 10
    Centers for Disease Control and Prevention and FDA Food Code, 10
    Centers for Disease Control and Prevention (CDC) top five reasons why food becomes unsafe, 15, 45, 66, 82, 98, 114, 126
CFR (Code of Federal Regulations)
    CFR and Federal law, 98
    CFR and game animal, 106, 121, 150
    CFR and poultry, 121, 151
Chemical
    Chemical labeling, 22
    Chemical safety, 74
    Chemical storage, 74, 102
    Chemical training, 90
Chemical Hazards
    Chemical hazards, defined, 22, 152
    Chemical hazards added to foods, 22
    Chemical hazards naturally occurring, 22
Children's Menu, 119
Chlorine
    Chlorine as a chemical sanitizer, 67-68
    Chlorine, Safety Data Sheet, 74
Ciguatoxin, 43
Class I, II, III food recalls, 101
Cleaners, 66
Cleaning
    Cleaning defined, 66, 152
    Cleaning food contact surfaces and equipment, 50-51
    Cleaning methods, 67
    Cleaning and PIC responsibilities, 12
    Cleaning premises, 50-57
    Cleaning and service animals, 132
    Cleaning warewashing and dishwashing machines, 70-71
    Cleaning vomit or fecal matter, 90
Clostridium botulinum, 40-41, 138
Clostridium perfringens, 40-41
CLs, *see* Critical Limits
Cold holding, 45, 69, 126
Comminuted, defined, 120, 152
Complex Food Preparation, 139-140
Conditional Employee
    Conditional Employee responsibility to report health illnesses, 12, 87
    Conditional Employee defined, 91-152
Confirmed disease outbreak, 10, 17, 152
Consumer Advisories, 119

Contact surfaces
    Contact surfaces and cross contamination, 53, 56-57
    Contact surfaces cleaning and sanitizing, 68-73
    Contact surfaces equipment, 71
Contamination
    Contamination and handling of food, 82-84, 101-103, 126, 131
    Contamination between raw and RTE or cooked food, 27
    Contamination by food-handlers or customers who are ill, 82-84
    Contamination chemical hazard, 22, 68
    Contamination defined, 29
    Contamination deliberate, 11
    Contamination and facility design, 52-53, 57
    Contamination food equipment and utensils, 51, 57, 67, 70-71
    Contamination and human waste, 55
    Contamination intentional, *see also* Food defense
    Contamination personal care items, 86, 91
    Contamination risk of, 72, 74
    Contamination and storage, 54, 71
    Contamination tasting foods, 85
    Contamination types, 66
    Contamination unintentional, *see also* Food safety
    Contamination vomit or fecal matter, 90
Continuous monitoring, 142-144, 152
Control measures, 73
Control point (CP), 141, 152
Controlled Atmosphere Packing (CAP), 138, 145, 152
Cook-chill (CC), 138, 145, 152
Cooking
    Cooking and food labeling, 98
    Cooking and food storage, 102
    Cooking does not kill the spore form of bacteria, 41
    Cooking foods and active managerial control, 45
    Cooking foods change oxygen environment, 26
    Cooking foods and consumer advisories, 119
    Cooking foods example, 45, 142
    Cooking foods and highly susceptible populations, 119
    Cooking foods and microwave cooking of raw animal foods, 116
    Cooking foods minimum internal temperature and time, 42, 114-115
    Cooking foods monitoring, 117
    Cooking foods and parasites, 41-42
    Cooking foods special considerations, 116
    Cooking foods to thaw, 104
    Cooking foods using non-continuous method, 116
    Cooking Method and Meat Roast Size Chart, 115
Cooling, 127-128, 152
Core Food Safety Features, 50-58, 152
Corrective action, 14, 143, 152
CP, *see* Control point
Crisis management, 14
Critical control point (CCP), 141-142, 145, 152
Critical limit (CL), 142, 145, 152
Cross-contact, 30, 152
Cross-contamination, 16, 70, 102-103, 131, 152
Cryptosporidium parvum, 42

Cryptosporidiosis, 42

D

Data plate, 70, 152
Date marking, 105
Department of Homeland Security, *see* United States Department of Homeland Security
Diarrhetic shellfish poisoning (DSP), 43
Disclosure, 119-120, 152
Documentation, *see* Record keeping (HACCP Principle 7)
Dry storage relative humidity, 102
Dry storage temperature, 102
DSP (diarrhetic shellfish poisoning), 43

E

E. coli, *see* Escherichia coli
Employee Accommodations, 86
Employee Health Management and Reportable Health Illnesses, 87-89
Employee, defined, 91, 153
Equipment
    Equipment and active managerial control, 15, 45
    Equipment cleaning and sanitizing of, 31, 66-71
    Equipment and core food safety features, 50-58
    Equipment and crisis management, 14
    Equipment and flow of food, 16
    Equipment and hazards, 22-23
    Equipment and person-in-charge, 12
    Equipment and pest control, 72-73
    Equipment and storage of clean equipment, 71
    Equipment and temperature, 28-29
Equivalent Cooking Time/Temperature Combinations Chart, 115
Escherichia coli (E. coli highly contagious), 40, 88-89
    Escherichia coli (E. coli), *see also* Hemorrhagic colitis
Exclude, 10, 39-40, 87, 89, 91
Exclude or Restrict Decision Tree, 89
Exterior areas, 52

F

Facility design, 50, 139
FATTOM, 25-27
FDA
    FDA ALERT, 11
    FDA Food Code, 10
    FDA and food defense, 11
    FDA and food standards, 98
    FDA defined, 153
    FDA References, 19, 34, 47, 62, 78-79, 93-94, 109-110, 123, 134, 147
    FDA, *see* United States Food and Drug Administration
First Aid and Other Personal Care Items, 86
First-in first-out (FIFO) food product rotation, 73, 102
Fish
    Fish as an allergen, 30, 32
    Fish cooking, 114, 116
    Fish defined, 106, 120, 153
    Fish documentation, 99, 118
    Fish food of special concern, 99

Fish and non-cooking destruction of pathogens, 42, 118
Fish receive, 100
Fish self-service, 131
Fish storing, 102
Fish and TCS foods, 27
Fish as toxins, 22
Flow of food, 16
Food additives, 138
Food allergy, *see also* Allergens, 12
Food and Drug Administration, *see* United States Food and Drug Administration
Food Code, 10, 153
Food Code Definitions, 17, 32, 45, 60, 76, 91, 106-107, 120-121, 132, 145
Food Code minimum lighting levels, 56
Food Code References, 19, 34, 47, 62, 78-79, 93-94, 109-110, 123, 134, 147
Food-contact surface, 68-71, 76, 153
Food defense, 11, 153
Food employee, defined, 17, 91, 153
Food equipment and utensils, 50-51
Food establishment, defined, 60, 153
Food For Thought
    Food For Thought: Americans with Disabilities Act, 87
    Food For Thought: Assisting Customers with Allergies, 31
    Food For Thought: Bacteria, 41
    Food For Thought: Cooling, 124
    Food For Thought: Developing Cooling Procedures, 128
    Food For Thought: Equipment, 51
    Food For Thought: Exclude or Restrict Decision Tree, 89
    Food For Thought: FATTOM, 26
    Food For Thought: Fish, 118
    Food For Thought: Juice Warning, 101
    Food For Thought: Record Keeping, 58
    Food For Thought: Reduced Oxygen Packaging (ROP), 138
    Food For Thought: Reduced Oxygen Packaging (ROP) Fish, 104
    Food For Thought: Service Animals, 132
    Food For Thought: Time as a Public Health Control, 126
    Food For Thought: Viruses, 39
    Food For Thought: Warewashing Water Temperatures, 71
    Food For Thought: Water Supply, 58
Food poisoning, 40
Food recalls, *see* recalls
Food safety
    Food safety and active managerial control, 15-16, 45
    Food safety and allergens, 30-31
    Food safety and core features, 50-59
    Food safety and crisis management, 14
    Food safety culture, 10
    Food safety defined, 11, 153
    Food safety hazards, 141-142
    Food safety and personal hygiene, 82-90
    Food safety and person-in-charge, 12
    Food safety regulations, 10
    Food safety training, 12-13, 90, 139
Food, defined, 106, 153
Foodborne illness, 10, 15, 153
Foodborne disease outbreak, 10, 17, 153

Foodborne illnesses
    Foodborne illnesses active managerial control, 15
    Foodborne illnesses Big 6, 10
    Foodborne illnesses causes, 38-40, 72, 82
    Foodborne illnesses death from, 10
    Foodborne illnesses defined, 10, 153
    Foodborne illnesses FATTOM, 26
    Foodborne illnesses prevention of, *see* Active managerial control
Foods of Special Concern, 99-100
Fruits, washing, 105
Fungi: Molds, Yeasts, and Mushrooms, 42, 153

G

Game animal
    Game animal approved supplier, 100
    Game animal defined, 106, 121, 153
    Game animal minimum internal cooking temperature and time, 114-115
Giardia lamblia, 42, 88
Giardiasis, 42
Glass (as physical hazards), 23, 56
Glove types, 83-84
Gloves
    Gloves and allergies, 31
    Gloves and avoid foodborne illness, 82
    Gloves as a utensil, 76, 83-84, 129
    Gloves as personal protective equipment, 66
Grade A standard, 106, 153
Ground beef, 40, 45, 69, 120, 141-142, 149

H

HACCP, 138, 153
HACCP overview, 138
HACCP plan
    HACCP plan defined, 138, 145, 153
    HACCP plan and variance, 99, 105, 138-139, 145
HACCP Principle 1: Conducting a Hazard Analysis, 141
HACCP Principle 2: Determine Critical Control Points, 141-142
HACCP Principle 3: Establish Critical Limits, 142
HACCP Principle 4: Establish Monitoring Procedures, 142-143
HACCP Principle 5: Identify Corrective Actions, 143
HACCP Principle 6: Verification, 143
HACCP Principle 7: Record Keeping and Documentation, 144
Hand antiseptics, 83
Hand care, 84
Handling (food), 13, 15-16, 23, 26, 50, 52, 82, 84, 87, 129, 131
Handwashing facilities, 54
Handwashing sink, 54, 60, 83, 153
Hazard(s), defined, 30, 153 *see also* specific types.
    Hazards, 22-23, 32, 42-43, 45, 141, 145
Hemorrhagic colitis, *see also* , Eschericha coli (E. coli)
Hepatitis A (highly contagious), 39, 87-88
Highly susceptible population (HSP), 23, 32, 153
Holding foods
    Holding foods and active managerial control, 15-16, 45
    Holding foods cold holding, 126
    Holding foods hot holding, 126

Hot and Cold Food Holding, 126
Hot holding, 126
How to clean and sanitize, 68-70
Hygiene, defined, *see also* Personal hygiene

I

Ice-point method, 29
Imminent health hazard, 14, 17, 153
Incubation, 120, 149
Infection, defined, 38, 153
Infection foodborne, 23, 38, 153
Infection toxin-mediated, 38, 155
Inspection
    Inspection and person-in-charge, 17, 66, 91
    Inspection and regulatory authority, 58, 98
    Inspection process, 13-14
Intentional contamination, 11
Interior Areas, 52-53
Interior Storage Areas, 54
Internal cooking temperatures, 42, 45, 114, 119
Intoxication, 38, 153
Iodine, as a chemical sanitizer, 67-68

J

Jaundice, 10, 39, 43, 87
Jewelry, 23, 82
Juice, 40, 98, 105-106, 153

K

Key Drop Delivery, 101

L

Labeling, 86, 98, 101-102, 105, 131-132
Latex, allergies to, 83
Lighting, 14, 56
Listeria monocytogenes, 23, 40, 53, 138, 145
Listeriosis, 23, 40

M

Major food allergen, 30, 32, 154
Manual warewashing and dishwashing, 70-71
MAP foods, *see* Modified atmosphere packing foods
Material Safety Data Sheets, 74
Meat defined, 107, 154
Mechanical tenderized, 114, 121, 154
Medicines, 74, 86, 91
Menu, 119
Microorganisms
    Microorganisms and active managerial control, 45
    Microorganisms bacteria, 40-41
    Microorganisms biological hazards, 22, 38
    Microorganisms causing foodborne illness, 10, 38
    Microorganisms disease-causing, 10
    Microorganisms FATTOM, 25
    Microorganisms fungi, 42
    Microorganisms parasites, 41-42
    Microorganisms toxins, 42-43
    Microorganisms viruses, 39

Microware, thawing foods in, 104
Microwave Cooking of Raw Animal Foods (fish, eggs, meat, and poultry), 116
Minimum Internal Cooking Temperatures and Times, 114-115
Modified atmosphere packaging (MAP) foods, 138, 145, 154
Moisture
    Moisture and TCS foods, 116
    Moisture content, 115
    Moisture and FATTOM, 25-26
    Moisture as it relates to food equipment and the facility, 51, 53
Molds, 38, 42
Molluscan shellfish, 99, 107, 118, 154
Monitoring
    Monitoring cooking temperatures, 117
    Monitoring continuous, 142, 149
    Monitoring establishing procedures for, 142-143
    Monitoring non-continuous, 142, 151
    Monitoring of time and temperature, 40-42
    Monitoring using thermometers, 28

N

Neurotoxic shellfish poisoning (NSP), 43
Non-Cooking Destruction of Pathogens, 118
Non-Continuous Cooking
    Non-continuous cooking procedure, 116
    Non-continuous cooking, defined, 121, 154
Non-continuous monitoring, 142-143, 154
Norovirus (highly contagious), 10, 39, 87-88, 90
NSF International seal of approval, 51
NSP (neurotoxin shellfish poisoning), 43

O

Oxygen
    Oxygen and FATTOM, 25-26
    Oxygen and Reduced Oxygen Packaging, 104, 138

P

Packaged, 30, 107, 130, 154
Packaging
    Packaging and an approved supplier, 98
    Packaging controlled atmosphere, 101, 145, 149
    Packaging food on display, 131
    Packaging inspection of, 40
    Packaging juice, 138
    Packaging modified atmosphere, 145, 151
    Packaging reduced oxygen, 104, 138
Parasites
    Parasite, defined, 41, 154
    Parasites non-cooking destruction, 118
    Parasites as biological hazards, 41-42
    Parasites game animals, 100
Pathogens
    Pathogens cross-contamination, 16
    Pathogens defined, 22
    Pathogens FATTOM and the growth of, 25-26
    Pathogens infections and toxin-mediated infections, 38
    Pathogens hazards, 22-23, 38-42
    Pathogens pest control, 67

Pathogens reduced, 67, 83, 114, 129
Pathogens sources, 39-43, 82, 84, 87, 99, 105
PCO, *see* Pest control operator
Person-in-charge, 12, 17, 91, 154
Personal care item, 74, 86, 154
Personal hygiene
    Personal hygiene and active managerial control, 15, 45
    Personal hygiene and bacteria, 40
    Personal hygiene and parasites, 41-42
    Personal hygiene and viruses, 39
    Personal hygiene practices, 82-86, 129
    Personal hygiene handwash facilities, 54
    Personal hygiene reportable health illnesses, 10, 87-89
Pest control 51-52, 72-74
Pest control operator (PCO), 73
Pesticides
    Pesticides and storage, 74
    Pesticides as a chemical hazard, 22
    Pesticides pest control system, 72-74
    Pesticides poisonous or toxic materials, 60, 76, 154
pH
    pH and FATTOM, 25-26
    pH defined, 32, 154
Physical hazards, 23, 82, 141, 154
Plan review, 50
Plastic (as physical hazard), 22-23, 66
Plumbing systems, 58, 154
Poisonous or toxic materials, 14, 54, 60, 76, 154
Potable water, 57-58, 103, 154
Poultry
    Poultry as a TCS food, 27
    Poultry cooking, 114
    Poultry defined, 121, 154
    Poultry food standards, 98
    Poultry microwave, 116
    Poultry receiving, 100
    Poultry self-service, 131
    Poultry source, 40
    Poultry storage, 102
Premises, defined, 60, 154
Prepare, 16, 105
Preparing, 31, 41, 103-104
Procedures for Responding to Contamination Events, 90
PSP (paralytic shellfish poisoning), 43
Purchase, 98-100
Purchasing
    Purchasing and active managerial control, 15, 45
    Purchasing and food defense, 11
    Purchasing flow of food, 16
    Purchasing from an approved source, 22-23, 98-100
    Purchasing prevention, 39-43
    Purchasing responsibility PIC, 42

Q

Quaternary ammonium compounds (quats), as a chemical sanitizer, 67-68

R

Ratite, 114, 121, 154
Raw food
    Raw food and customers, 12, 41
    Raw food as a food source, 40, 42, 99
    Raw food clean and sanitize, 69
    Raw food consumer advisory, 12, 119
    Raw food cooking, 116
    Raw food disclosure, 120, 149
    Raw food non-cooking, 118
    Raw food pathogens, 105
    Raw food preventing cross-contamination, 16
    Raw food reminder, 154
    Raw food self-service areas, 131
    Raw food storage of, 102
    Raw food wash hands and change gloves, 82
Re-service, 130, 132, 154
Ready-to-eat (RTE) food
    Ready-to-eat (RTE) bare hand contact with, 16, 84
    Ready-to-eat (RTE) clean and sanitize, 69
    Ready-to-eat (RTE) food defined, 27, 154
    Ready-to-eat (RTE) food source, 39-40
    Ready-to-eat (RTE) preventing cross-contamination, 16
    Ready-to-eat (RTE) reheating, 128
    Ready-to-eat (RTE) self-service areas and, 131
    Ready-to-eat (RTE) storage, 102
    Ready-to-eat (RTE) using suitable utensils, 12, 129
Recalls, 101
Receiving deliveries
    Receiving deliveries first-in first-out, 102
    Receiving deliveries flow of food, 16
    Receiving deliveries inspect food, 23, 101
    Receiving deliveries supplier documentation, 42, 99
Record keeping (HACCP Principle 7), 144
Reduced Oxygen Packaging (ROP), 138
Refrigerated Food Storage Practices, 102
Refrigerator
    Refrigerator cooling, 127
    Refrigerator personal care items, 86
    Refrigerator storage, 102
    Refrigerator thawing foods in, 104
Regulatory authority
    Regulatory authority and person-in-charge, 12
    Regulatory authority and the establishment, 58
    Regulatory authority approved sources, 98
    Regulatory authority and HACCP, 138
    Regulatory authority non-continuous cooking, 116
    Regulatory authority reportable diseases, 87
    Regulatory authority variance, 138, 145, 155
Reheating, 128
Reminder, 119, 121, 154
Reportable Health Illnesses, 10, 87
Restrict
    Restrict defined, 87, 91, 155
    Restrict employees, 10, 87-89
Risk, defined, 32, 43, 45, 155

Risk factors, 15, 45, 66, 82, 98, 114, 126
Roast, time/temperature ranges for, 114-115
ROP, *see* Reduced oxygen packaging,
RTE food, *see* Ready-to-eat food

S

Safety, *see* Food safety
Salmonella
    Salmonella nontyphoidal 10, 87-89
    Salmonella species, 40
    Salmonella typhi (typhimurium), 10, 40, 87-88
    Salmonellosis (salmonella) highly contagious, 40, 45
Same-Day, 139-140
Sanitation
    Sanitation and cleanliness, 50, 53
    Sanitation and equipment, 51
    Sanitation and pest control, 73
    Sanitation and physical condition, 50
    Sanitation chemicals, 22
    Sanitation features 13, 52
Sanitization
    Sanitization defined, 76, 155
    Sanitization warewashing, 70
Sanitizing
    Sanitizing and cleaning, 66-69
    Sanitizing and wiping cloths, 69-70
    Sanitizing chemical, 67-68
    Sanitizing defined, 155
    Sanitizing heat, 67
    Sanitizing warewashing and dishwashing machines, 70-71
Scombrotoxin, 43
Self-Service Areas, 131
Service animal, 132, 155
Service Sinks for Disposal of Liquid Cleaning Waste, 55
Serving Food, 129
Serving Food Off-Site, 131-132
Shellfish toxins, 22, 42-43
Shellstock, 99, 107, 155
Shigella, 10, 40-41, 87-89
Shigellosis highly contagious, 40
Shucked shellfish, 99, 107, 155
Simple/No-Cook recipes, 139-140
Slacking, 104, 107, 155
Smoking, Eating, and Drinking, 84
SOPs, *see* Standard operating procedures
Sous vide (SV), defined, 138, 145, 155
Special Cooking Considerations, 116
Specifications
    Specifications equipment, 57
    Specifications manufactures, 29, 67, 70
    Specifications purchasing, 100, 144
Spore former, 41
Standard operating procedures (SOPs), 38, 144
Staphylococcus aureus, 40-41, 82, 88
Storage, 54-59, 68, 73-74, 101-102, 118
Storage of chemicals, 66, 74
Storage of clean equipment, 71
Storage chemicals, 102

Storing, 59, 70, 86, 101-102
Structural Components of the Establishment, 59-52
Suppliers approved, 39, 42-43, 98-100
SV, *see* Sous vide

T

Tasting food, 85
TCS, *see* Time/temperature control for safety of food
TDZ, *see* Temperature danger zone
Temperature control (TC) 69, 98, 102, 104, 126
Temperature danger zone (TDZ), 25, 27
    Temperature danger zone, a process approach, 139
    Temperature danger zone (TDZ), cold holding, 126
    Temperature danger zone (TDZ), hot holding, 126
    Temperature danger zone (TDZ), properly thaw foods, 104
    Temperature danger zone (TDZ), serving, 129
Temperature measuring device, 28-29
Temperature, *see also* Time/temperature control for safety of food
Thawing foods, 104
Thermometers, 28
Thermometers calibrating, 29
Time
    Time and chemical contact, 68, 71
    Time and FATTOM, 25-26
    Time and onset of illness, 40, 42-43
    Time as a critical limit, 40, 42-43, 70, 142
Time as a Public Health Control, 126, 155
Time temperature abuse, 16, 101, 103-104, 131, 155
Time/Temperature Control for Safety of Food – TCS Foods, 27, 40, 45, 104, 114, 119, 127-128, 131, 155
Toilet Rooms, 55
Toxins
    Toxins and chemical hazards, 22
    Toxins and time/temperature control for safety, 25, 40-42, 127
    Toxins and toxin-mediated infections, 38, 155
    Toxins: Mushroom Toxins, Fish Toxins, Shellfish Toxins, and Plant Toxins, 22, 42-43, 99-100
Training, 13, 90, 139
Two-stage cooling, 127-128
Typhoid fever, *see* Salmonellosis (salmonella), 40

U

U. S. Department of Agriculture (USDA), 107, 155
    U. S. Department of Agriculture (USDA) and food standards, 98
    U. S. Department of Agriculture (USDA) and Food Code, 10
UL seals of approval, 51
Unintentional contamination, 11
United Stated Food and Drug Administration (FDA), *see also* FDA Food Code
United States Department of Health and Human Services (HHS) and Food Code, 10
Unsafe food, 98
USDA, *see* U. S. Department of Agriculture
Utensil, 28, 50-54, 66-71, 76, 83-85, 103, 129, 131-132, 155

V

Vacuum packed (VP), 138, 145, 155
Variance, 138-139, 145, 155

Ventilation System, 53, 57, 155
Verification (HACCP Principles 6), 143, 155
Vibrio, 88, 99
Virus
    Virus as biological hazards, 22, 38
    Virus control of, 39
    Virus defined, 155
    Virus game animals, 100
    Virus shellfish, 99
Vomit or fecal matter, 90
VP, *see* Vacuum packing

W

Warewashing, defined, 76, 155
Warewashing and dishwashing machines, 70
Washing hands, 82-89
Waste and Recyclable Facilities and Equipment, 59
Water activity (a_w)
    Water activity (a_w) as a critical limit, 142
    Water activity (a_w) defined, 32, 152
    Water activity (a_w) for growth and pathogens, 25
Water supply, 50, 57-58
Water, thawing foods in, 104
When to clean and sanitize, 69
Whole-muscle, intact beef, 121, 155
Wood, 66
Work attire, 82

X

Y

Yersinia enterocolitica, 88

Z

Quick Reference Guide

Hazards
- Biological
- Chemical
- Physical

Hand Washing
1. Wet hands using water that is at least 100°F (37.8°C)
2. Apply Soap
3. Scrub for 10-15 seconds
4. Rinse
5. Dry

Seven HACCP Principles
1. Conduct a Hazard Analysis
2. Determine Critical Control Points
3. Establish Critical Limits
4. Establish Monitoring Procedures
5. Establish Corrective Actions
6. Verification
7. Record Keeping and Documentation

Cleaning vs. Sanitizing
- Cleaning removes soil
- Sanitizing reduces pathogens

Report HENSSS
- **H**epatitis A
- **E**. coli shiga toxin-producing
- **N**orovirus
- **S**higella
- **S**almonella typhi
- **S**almonella nontyphoidal

CDC Top Five Risk Factors
1. Purchasing food from unsafe sources
2. Failing to cook food adequately
3. Holding food at incorrect temperatures
4. Using contaminated equipment
5. Practicing poor personal hygiene

Temperature Requirements
Temperature Danger Zone (TDZ): 41°F - 135°F (5°C - 57.2°C)

Most Dangerous Section of the TDZ: 70°F - 125°F (21.1°C - 51.7°C)

Hot Holding: 135°F (57.2°C) or higher

Cold Holding: 41°F (5°C) or lower

Cooling: 135°F to 70°F (57.2°C to 21.1°C) within 2 hours
70°F to 41°F (21.1°C to 5°C) within 4 hours

Water Temperatures
212°F (100°C): boiling-point calibration
180°F (82.2°C): dishwashing machine hot water sanitizing
171°F (77.2°C): hot water for sanitizing
110°F (43.3°C): dishwashing
100°F (37.8°C): handwashing
70°F (21.1°C): running water for thawing
32°F (0°C): ice-point calibration

Minimum Internal Cooking Temperature
- 165°F (73.9°C) – Poultry, Stuffed, Reheated, Microwave food
- 155°F (68.3°C) – Ground Meat, Ground Seafood, Eggs-hot held
- 145°F (62.8°C) – Meat, Seafood, Eggs-for immediate service
- 135°F (57.2°C) – Heat-treated plant foods, Commercially processed food

Food Defense ALERT
- **A**ssure
- **L**ook
- **E**mployees
- **R**eports
- **T**hreats

FATTOM
- **F**ood
- **A**cidity
- **T**emperature
- **T**ime
- **O**xygen
- **M**oisture

Flow of Food: Purchase → Receive → Store → Prepare → Cook → Hold → Cool → Reheat → Serve